LEADING IN
SYNC

LEADING IN SYNC

Teacher Leaders and Principals Working Together for Student Learning

JILL HARRISON BERG

Alexandria, Virginia USA

1703 N. Beauregard St. • Alexandria, VA 22311-1714 USA
Phone: 800-933-2723 or 703-578-9600 • Fax: 703-575-5400
Website: www.ascd.org • E-mail: member@ascd.org
Author guidelines: www.ascd.org/write

Deborah S. Delisle, *Executive Director*; Stefani Roth, *Publisher*; Genny Ostertag, *Director, Content Acquisitions*; Susan Hills, *Acquisitions Editor*; Julie Houtz, *Director, Book Editing & Production*; Joy Scott Ressler, *Editor*; Judi Connelly, *Associate Art Director*; Lauren Lapid, *Graphic Designer*; Electronic Quill, *Typesetter*; Mike Kalyan, *Director, Production Services*; Shajuan Martin, *E-Publishing Specialist*; Sue Curran, *Production Specialist*.

Author photo taken by Max Geissbühler.

All web links in this book are correct as of the publication date below but may have become inactive or otherwise modified since that time. If you notice a deactivated or changed link, please e-mail books@ascd.org with the words "Link Update" in the subject line. In your message, please specify the web link, the book title, and the page number on which the link appears.

PPAPERBACK ISBN: 978-1-4166-2647-3   ASCD product #118021   n8/18
PDF E-BOOK ISBN: 978-1-4166-2698-5

Quantity discounts are available: e-mail programteam@ascd.org or call 800-933-2723, ext. 5773, or 703-575-5773. For desk copies, go to www.ascd.org/deskcopy.

Library of Congress Cataloging-in-Publication Data
Name: Berg, Jill Harrison, author.
Title: Leading in sync : teacher leaders and principals working together for
    student learning / Jill Harrison Berg.
Description: Alexandria, VA, USA: ASCD, [2018] | Includes bibliographical
    references and index.
Identifiers: LCCN 2018018950 | ISBN 9781416626473 (pbk.)
Subjects: LCSH: Teacher-principal relationships—United States. |
    Teachers—Professional relationships—United States. | Educational
    leadership—United States.
Classification: LCC LB2832.2.B47 2018 | DDC 371.1/06—dc23 LC
record available at https://lccn.loc.gov/2018018950

26 25 24 23 22 21 20 19 18   1 2 3 4 5 6 7 8 9 10 11 12

LEADING IN SYNC

Teacher Leaders and Principals Working Together for Student Learning

JILL HARRISON BERG

Foreword

When I work with schools, a question I often ask teachers is, "Who are the teacher leaders in this school?" There is rarely any hesitancy in the answer. The same two or three names come to the surface time and time again, even though they may have no official leadership position in the school. "Why are they teacher leaders, in your view?" I then ask. Again, the answers are fairly consistent—because they have widely recognized expertise as classroom teachers, because they are respectful of their colleagues, because they work incredibly hard, and because they are in it for the students, not for themselves or their own careers.

But ask teachers in general about the virtue or value of having teacher leaders and all kinds of concerns will rise to the surface. Will they swap sides to join the administration? Why should they be paid more if they are not obviously better than anybody else? Shouldn't teachers be rewarded for doing better work in the classroom instead of taking on jobs outside it?

For a long time, teachers and their professional associations have been at best ambivalent about teacher leadership. This is odd because the original Latin word for "education" comes from the Latin *educare,* meaning "to lead out." All teachers are already leading, whether they like it or not. So if it's OK to lead children, why should leading colleagues be a problem?

Jill Harrison Berg has been a teacher leader and helped to prepare great numbers of teacher leaders herself. She is no innocent when it comes to the issues. She's heard all the objections from administrators, unions, and teachers themselves. But from the research, including her own on what motivates teachers and keeps them going in the job, and through years of working with teacher leaders in courses and consultancies, often with very challenging schools, Jill has learned why teacher leadership matters, how it can make all teachers become better, and how this helps the students in our schools.

Jill sets out a compelling case for teacher leadership in full awareness of all the objections to it. She provides compelling cases of improvement and turnaround where teacher leadership has come to the fore. She provides practical tools and protocols to help teachers support each other as teacher leaders. She builds on the assets of what teachers have rather than perseverating on what they allegedly lack. She highlights beautiful moments when teachers see, in the work of their leadership, the chance for their colleagues to shine. But she also demonstrates that effective teacher leadership doesn't only rest on structures and protocols; it also depends on the willingness and ability to establish trust and solidarity within the teacher community and with the administration of the district or the school.

In my own work across the world, including our latest study of collaborative professionalism among teachers (Hargreaves & O'Connor, 2018), I've seen the power of honest feedback that teachers can give to each other in environments of openness and trust. I've witnessed how teachers learn to give up the idea that they are the boss of everything in their own classes when they start planning curriculum innovations with colleagues in other schools. I've seen teachers seize the leadership of professional learning communities from their principals and then see the principals thank them for it. We know what teacher leadership can do and we know what it looks like when teachers really know how to do it. Here, Jill also shows you, concretely, practically, and realistically, how you can help develop other teacher leaders and become a better teacher leader yourself.

The world needs newer, better, greater leadership from the many, not bad leadership by a few. The best place to begin that movement is in our schools. Jill Harrison Berg's book is a great step forward in that overdue direction.

—Andy Hargreaves
Research Professor, Lynch School of Education, Boston College
President, International Congress of School Effectiveness & Improvement
Editor-in-Chief, *Journal of Professional Capital & Community*

Acknowledgments

This book is built on lessons learned directly from teachers, principals, and other school leaders who were generous and trusting enough to open up to me about what made teacher leadership so enticing to them, yet too often so painfully hard.

Most of these stories came directly through my experience developing and directing the Boston Teacher Leadership Certificate (BTLC) Program. I am indebted to Ellen Guiney and the Boston Plan for Excellence for giving me the opportunity and encouragement to create the program, and to John D'Auria and Teachers21 for supporting its expansion beyond Boston. From 2010 through now, more than 200 teachers from the Boston and Arlington Public Schools have participated in our practice-based leadership development courses designed and facilitated by teachers, and several other locales have created programs based on our model. Throughout these courses, teachers are asked to report what makes it easy or hard for them to implement the ideas and strategies they are learning in class. It was through reviewing each year's data, often together with the BTLC governing board of teachers, and reflecting on it in light of my coaching experiences with principals, that many of the ideas and tools in this book were born. I appreciate the honesty of these 200+ teachers, who I will refrain from naming individually here, and I am exceptionally grateful for the wisdom and dedication of past and present members of the BTLC governing board of teachers, who I am compelled to identify by name: Sean Brooks, Christy Connolly, Nicole Davis, Andrea Devine, Katie Lyons, Courtney Keegan, Jennifer Lambertz, Nina Lessin-Joseph, Julie Wang McCarthy, Lauren McDade, Frank Pantano, Noah Patel, Xavier Rozas, Ariana Sicairos-McCarthy, Doris Van Gorder McGoff, Alice Wong-Tucker, and Carla Zils.

The solutions-oriented perspective I have taken to these teacher leaders' challenges has been informed by my experiences working with school leadership teams over the past 25 years. I learned about the importance of shared vision and core values from principal Lynn Stuart and my many amazing colleagues while working as a teacher leader at the Cambridgeport School in Cambridge, Massachusetts. The instructional leadership team at Boston's Mary E. Curley Middle School, and especially principal Gerardo Martinez and literacy coach Lydia Torres, informed my ideas about tools and structures that could increase shared ownership of the school's improvement work. Several Boston schools have experimented with having the entire Instructional Leadership Team or even the full faculty participate together in BTLC courses or in summer institutes based on BTLC content. The feedback from educators in these schools, including Henry Grew Elementary School, Donald McKay K–8 School, Excel High School, Mather Elementary School, Mattahunt Elementary School, Channing Elementary School, and Lilla G. Frederick Pilot Middle School, was invaluable in helping me to think more deeply about the symptoms and strategies for addressing systems misalignment.

I was able to further deepen my understanding of teacher leadership from a systems perspective through my role as an advisor and faculty member for the Network to Transform Teaching, and I am appreciative of Emma Parkerson, Joe Doctor, Lisa Clarke, and Peggy Brookins from the National Board for Professional Teaching Standards (NBPTS) for including me as a key partner in this work. In this national project, cross-stakeholder teams from 10 states have used the principles of improvement science from the Carnegie Foundation for the Advancement of Teaching to form a networked improvement community committed to testing the roles National Board Certified Teachers and the NBPTS body of knowledge on accomplished teaching might play in raising public expectations about what good teaching is and the viability of all children having access to it. Again, the full list of individuals from whose thinking I benefited is far too long to include here, as it includes school, district, and state-level leaders from these 10 states: Alabama, Arizona, California, Illinois, Kentucky, Nevada, New Mexico, New York, North Carolina, and Washington. However, two sites invited me in for a deeper dive and to think with them about the particular puzzles and possibilities in their states. For this, I am especially grateful to Suzanne Farmer in Kentucky, and Colleen McDonald and Annette Romano in New York.

My interpretations of these experiences have been informed by research. I am thankful for the first-class research training I received as a research assistant with Susan Moore Johnson and the Project on the Next Generation of Teachers while earning my doctorate at Harvard's Graduate School of Education, and I am grateful for the research that has come from the community of colleagues associated with this important research project. In addition, my ongoing research collaboration and friendship with Melinda Mangin and Cynthia Carver, including our partnership to establish a home for researchers of teacher leadership within the American

Educational Research Association, has helped to push my thinking in ways that I both appreciate and enjoy.

Finally, I would like to thank the many supporters and cheerleaders I have had throughout the development of this manuscript. Sonia Caus Gleason, Ellen Guiney, Linda Hanson, Amika Kemmler-Ernst, and Nina Lessin-Joseph generously read drafts and gave their time to serve as critical friends, providing important insights that helped to make this a better book. Kristina Hals, Cara Hill, Julie Duffield, and ASCD editor Susan Hills played essential roles in keeping me going during the writing process and reminding me that this was important. My father-in-law, Tom Berg, was an invaluable thought partner as I navigated key puzzles, while my parents, Roger and Marylyn Harrison, and my children, Althea and Maceo Berg, encouraged me with love. Last, and most significantly, my husband, Erik, not only provided insightful, honest, and specific feedback on multiple drafts, but he made sure I was supported, well-fed, and keeping my balance during the entire writing process. I am truly blessed to have such a generous, caring, and intelligent partner in the co-performance of life.

Introduction

The term *teacher leadership* has a nice ring to it. Teachers hear the term and imagine ways they could make a bigger difference beyond their own classrooms. Principals hear the term and hope they might be able to improve teachers' engagement and retention while getting some welcome help. Both imagine that this new partnership will be good for teacher satisfaction, school improvement, and reduction of principal burnout. Most significantly, they recognize that teacher leadership holds tremendous promise for improving the quality of teaching and raising student learning to new heights. The ugly truth is that although these important outcomes are possible, they are not at all likely without a commitment from both teachers and principals to work together on developing the knowledge, skills, and dispositions needed to work in concert. They must learn to co-perform leadership.

Effective co-performance of leadership requires teachers and principals to be on the same page about the vision they are trying to create, their understanding of the complementary roles each will play to reach that vision, and the trust required to make it work. Without such alignment, they will inadvertently work against each other, make each other frustrated, stymie school improvement progress, and lose precious energy that could be channeled into greater student success.

Maybe one of the following scenarios is familiar:

You're a teacher   Your principal asks you to be the team leader for your common planning team. You're excited about the opportunity and take time throughout the week crafting an agenda that will engage your colleagues. The night before the first team meeting, your principal e-mails you an agenda with a supportive note and thanks you for agreeing to implement it.

You're a principal	Committed to supporting your novice teachers, you observe them regularly and provide them with growth-oriented feedback in each of your district's Four Domains of Effective Teaching. The mentor you assign structures his support around the Six Dimensions of Quality Teaching from his coach training program. You later learn that the novice teacher is creating two sets of lesson plans before each observation.
You're a teacher	As your school's appointed math facilitator, you attend district meetings where you learn about useful resources you can bring back to your school. With no protected time to meet with math teachers, you decide to prepare a monthly e-mail to provide colleagues with key information and linked articles. At year-end, you ask some colleagues about the utility of your e-mails. They honestly explain, "We can't take on more that is not mandated by the administration."
You're a principal	You are happy to be named the new principal of a school with many formal teacher leader roles in place. The individuals holding those roles take great pride in them and count on the stipend they have received for many years. As you get to know the teachers and the important functions of each role, you see other teachers whose expertise would be a better match for those roles and who desire teacher leadership opportunities. Those teachers leave the building as soon as school dismisses in order to participate in external teacher leadership opportunities: a local policy fellowship, a district curriculum-writing project, and a university-based action-research project.

There is no "bad guy" in any of these scenarios, but it likely didn't feel that way to these educators at the time. One can imagine feelings of frustration, confusion, betrayal, and even anger that can lead teachers and principals alike to decide it may not be worth the extra effort. It would be much easier for the principal to avoid the hassle and just call the shots. It would be much more comfortable for a teacher to just keep their head down and mouth closed. But why the disconnect when both are well-intentioned?

The disconnect is not surprising when we consider how easy it is for teachers and administrators to be out of touch with what the other's job requires them to know and do. Most school and district administrators acquire the knowledge base on leadership in departments of educational administration within institutions of higher education, far removed from schools and the teachers with whom they will be expected to work. Then, once they are in schools, the structure of their work, isolated from peers with similar roles, means that they are drawn away from their teachers when it is time to engage in professional learning about leadership. Meanwhile, due to the rapid pace of change in the education context, any prior knowledge they may have had about the daily demands of being a classroom teacher rapidly becomes outdated.

Teachers, for their part, are largely on their own to pursue the knowledge base on leadership. Although teachers are leaders of their classrooms every day and stand to have a powerful leadership influence on their colleagues, the knowledge base on leadership is not traditionally considered part of the teacher education curriculum. Increasingly, institutions of higher education are offering graduate programs in teacher leadership, although they don't tend to integrate teachers with other school leaders. While the proliferation of these programs is tied to the introduction of teacher leadership endorsements offered today in dozens of states, such degrees and endorsements are neither a requirement nor a guarantee that the bearer will hold a formal teacher leader role at the school or district level. Participants, then, gain no particular advantage over other teachers in understanding what a school principal actually does all day, and how their unique skills and experiences might complement it.

Thus, today's teachers and principals largely learn about leadership while separate from each other and separate from their school contexts. This makes no sense. Principals and teacher leaders who are committed to improving schools together should invest in learning to lead together. Their shared commitment to leadership learning will model the learning culture that schools need, it will support them to develop shared understandings and language for their leadership practice, and it will facilitate their ability to co-perform leadership skillfully and stay in sync.

Most important, teachers and principals each bring to the table distinct and complementary knowledge, skills, and job functions. Schools serve students better when the strengths of both are maximized. To be sure, school and district administrators have a higher level of responsibility due to the positional authority of their roles. They are in control of more of the factors that influence this system than teachers are, and their role in evaluating teachers creates a power dynamic that cannot be overlooked. However, teachers and principals each have different perspectives on the school and they have different skill sets. They have distinct relationships with colleagues and distinct roles in supporting teaching and learning, the school's core work. These complementary differences create potential for better, more well-informed decision making, but they also suggest that co-performing leadership might take some practice and coordination.

The fact is, it takes two to tango. This book is a dancing lesson.

The ideas in this book were informed by over 25 years of teacher leadership research and practice and, principally, my role as founding director of the Boston Teacher Leadership Certificate (BTLC) Program. In 2010, I was offered a design challenge: to think about how teachers in the Boston Public Schools might have access to more powerful professional learning experiences. At that time, many Boston teachers reported that job-embedded professional time was frequently used for meetings, not learning, and the opportunities offered by the district were not as timely, sustained, or relevant to their immediate practice as they would like. At the same time, there was significant variation in student success across Boston's 130 schools. As a strategic partner of the Boston Public Schools, the Boston Plan for Excellence received a grant to respond to this concern. If teachers were tapped as professional learning leaders, could they be supported to share their expertise and grow their collective knowledge base in ways that would benefit student learning across all schools?

In fact, teachers were already at work as leaders in many job-embedded ways within the Boston Public Schools. In 2010, I documented over two dozen formal and informal roles that positioned teachers to influence the quality of teaching and learning beyond their own classrooms. Some teachers held a formally designated role such as mentor, team leader, or content specialist (e.g., literacy coach, math facilitator), while others influenced their colleagues' teaching without a designated role, such as by informally creating book study groups, participating in schoolwide teams, or stepping forward to offer professional development for colleagues. Yet, there was great variation in the presence of these roles across schools, and possibly even greater variation in teachers' effectiveness in these roles. These teachers had few, if any, opportunities to strengthen their leadership skills, share the tools and strategies they had developed with others holding the same role, or grow their collective knowledge base on how to perform these roles skillfully. Support from administrators was also rare, as they often were unaware of what teachers were actually doing in these roles.

I convened a group of teachers with diverse teacher leadership experience and supported them to create the BTLC Program, a series of teacher-led, graduate-credit-bearing courses designed to help teachers strengthen the leadership skills they need for teacher leader roles. We started small and embedded data routines into the work that could support the program to evolve in a way that was responsive to teachers' and schools' needs. The program's governing board of teachers met regularly to review the data, collaborate on program improvement, and identify obstacles.

As more and more teachers participated in the courses, we saw that many participating teacher leaders thrived in their work, felt renewed as professionals, and attributed specific student and school improvement gains to their learning. However, other teacher leaders became increasingly disgruntled and left their teacher leader roles, their schools, or even the profession. We realized we had been preparing teachers to be leaders of schools where somebody was already serving as leader. These other leaders (that is, principals)—whether thrilled or threatened by teachers' strengthened leadership skills—were often unsure how to respond.

Program data began to reveal patterns in the conditions that support or limit the promise of teacher leadership for student learning, and led me to develop a collection of tools and resources that could help principals and teacher leaders learn to lead together. The collection began to grow, and in 2013, after moving with the BTLC Program to Teachers21, an education nonprofit outside Boston, I began to experiment with these tools throughout Massachusetts and beyond. From New York to Kentucky to Iowa to New Mexico, these ideas, tools, and resources resonated with teachers and principals who were committed to the idea of teacher leadership but struggled to get the dance steps right. They are presented in this book.

Who is this book for? It is for all of the educators who influence teaching and learning in a school. This includes the principal, assistant principals, coaches, department leaders, grade-level and content team leaders, mentors, professional development leaders, and, in fact, all teachers. Each of these educators interacts with other educators in the school, and in doing so, each deliberately or unwittingly influences others' professional practice. They are all part of a school's leadership system, and they must learn to co-perform leadership together.

Since from a distributed perspective all teachers are leaders, and since in a learning organization all leaders are teachers (of adults), I've adopted the term *teacher/ leaders* to refer to this wide array of educators throughout this book. Admittedly the slash is awkward at first, but it serves as a constant reminder throughout the book of the truly hybrid nature of today's education roles and of the need to start thinking collectively about the leadership development of teachers and principals. The term *teacher leader* (sans slash) is used occasionally in this book to refer specifically to teachers who intend or are perceived to influence their colleagues' instruction.

Although district and state leaders, school partners, higher education faculty, and students of educational leadership will also benefit from the vision of shared leadership this book provides, it is intended primarily to provide teams of teacher/ leaders with the ideas and tools they need to practice co-performance of leadership with skill.

Chapter 1 explores how and why teacher leadership is so essential in schools that aim for all students to succeed. Schools committed to equity simply cannot justify being organized in ways that allow each student's experience to be informed only by the professional expertise of the few teachers to whom they are assigned. This chapter guides readers to recognize the ways in which leadership is already distributed in their contexts and to consider how they might maximize the differentiated and complementary expertise of teacher/leaders for accelerating student learning throughout the school by working in sync.

Chapter 2 emphasizes the role of a shared vision in synchronizing teacher/leaders' efforts. Often teacher/leaders are challenged to articulate their vision or to communicate about it effectively across roles. In this chapter, readers will encounter tools and strategies that teacher/leaders can experiment with together to help them come to a shared vision and communicate about it.

Chapter 3 invites readers to consider their shared vision in the context of current reality. Teacher/leaders are already influencing teaching and learning throughout their schools in intentional and unintentional ways. Thinking about these influences with regard to key leadership functions and essential priorities allows us to identify the gaps and redundancies, the needs and opportunities. It challenges teacher/leaders to think critically about the differentiated expertise teacher/leaders bring, who should be doing what, and how they might be supported to strengthen needed leadership skills.

Chapter 4 focuses on coordinating teacher/leaders' efforts. It offers key ideas and resources teacher/leaders can use to create a culture of teacher leadership throughout a school, as well as to create teams and roles designed to function in sync. The planning maps and communication routines provided here will support teacher/leaders' efforts to complement each other and to result in stronger organizational learning.

Chapter 5 discusses trust, the critical foundation required for this work. Chapters 2, 3, and 4 introduce ideas that may represent major changes to the way teacher/leaders work and communicate, requiring them to make compromises and possibly think differently about who they are as leaders. Teacher/leaders will be unwilling to do any of this without trust. Chapter 5 provides background research on how trust is built so that readers can understand the deliberate steps they can take toward strengthening and safeguarding trust.

Chapter 6 contains vignettes from four schools that have used the ideas and tools in this book to significant success. It is meant to illustrate what these ideas look like in action and to inspire leaders in their shared commitment to try some of these ideas together.

Each chapter begins with questions teacher/leaders can use to reflect individually and together about their context before engaging in the chapter content. Chapters 2, 3, 4, and 5, which each begin with a school-based scenario, conclude with reflection questions designed to support readers to envision the application of chapter themes in their own setting. My aim is to launch a conversation among teacher/leaders that, with the help of these resources, can extend far beyond this book.

Leadership as Influence

IN YOUR CONTEXT...

- To what extent are students benefiting from the expertise of the whole faculty, instead of just those teachers to whom they are assigned?
- In what formal and informal ways do teachers influence the quality of one another's teaching?
- How effectively is your school maximizing its leadership capacity?

The job of a school principal used to be like that of a ship's captain: monitoring the boat from the bridge and sending orders down the chain of command. The captain might have risen up through the ranks, developing familiarity with the route and most of the boat's roles until ultimately taking command of the boat or transferring from a ship that was likely quite similar.

Today, this metaphor no longer applies. Instead of an ocean, we're facing a river that is constantly changing course and moving at a quick pace. Navigation calls for a more efficient and responsive vessel. An effective principal might choose a crew boat, requiring all to take up an oar and in which each teammate has a unique role. As teammates practice their moves, they'll hone their ability to stay in sync, oars moving in together and out together, effectively and efficiently gliding toward victory. Just as crew boats strategically maximize the skills of each individual on board, today's effective schools strategically maximize the leadership influence of teachers.

Leadership for All Students

I'd like to believe that all students will learn at high levels. Honestly, this is hard to do while recognizing that high-level learning requires access to a kind of teaching that most U.S. schools are not organized to provide. In most U.S. schools, an elementary student's entire learning experience each year depends on the one teacher to whom the student is assigned for the year. If one 3rd grade teacher has strengths in science education and the one next door has a passion for teaching writing, by design, students will benefit from one or the other, but not both. Our schools do not acknowledge—or capitalize on—natural variation in strengths of teaching practice and teachers' expertise.

Middle and high school students are not much better off. If my son's 10th grade math teacher is new to the profession, absent with a family emergency, or simply has not mastered the vast array of knowledge and skills required of this year's new curriculum, my son may miss his one chance to engage deeply—and possibly fall in love with—the year's math content, even though a teacher with deep mathematical expertise may be next door. Some percentage of teachers will *always* be new or absent, and in today's information age, teachers will always have new areas to grow their teaching knowledge and professional practice. Currently, our system is not designed with this variation in mind.

In fact, the problem is even worse, given that in addition to developing subject area knowledge, we want today's students to develop 21st century skills, be college and career ready, and be happy and healthy. We also want their learning to be personalized and engaging and to take place in a safe and welcoming environment that maximizes technology for authentic learning. It's easy to see that the current system, in which students benefit from only a limited number of educators, cannot guarantee such an experience for every student. Some students will *always* be underserved by this system. The system controlling access to high-quality teaching and learning today is a lottery. Thus, we have inequitable outcomes by design.

We know that the quality of teaching is the most important school-based influence on student learning, and school leadership is the most important influence on the quality of teaching in a school. In this book, we explore how school leadership systems might be reconceived to maximize their influence on the quality of teaching and, thereby, on student learning.

The traditional view is that school administrators influence teachers and teachers influence students. This model positions teachers' expertise as a classroom-based asset and overlooks the potential value of teachers' expertise as a schoolwide asset. This would be fine if it were possible for school administrators to have mastery of the entire knowledge base on teaching required in a school, yet the range of teaching expertise required across a single school is simply too vast (see Figure 1.1).

FIGURE 1.1 RANGE OF TEACHING KNOWLEDGE AND SKILLS REQUIRED WITHIN A TYPICAL HIGH SCHOOL

Pedagogical Knowledge and Skills	Content Knowledge

• Understanding early adolescents
• Understanding young adults
• Understanding human development
• Understanding individual students
• Understanding special student subgroup populations in the school
• Gaining insight about students through partnerships with families
• Applying knowledge of students to build positive relationships
• Recognizing and capitalizing on students' diversity, commonalities, and talents
• Creating a learning environment in which fairness, equity, and diversity are modeled, taught, and practiced
• Adapting instruction and resources for fairness, equity, and diversity
• Maintaining safe and positive learning environments for all students
• Creating and capitalizing on educational settings
• Fostering and monitoring the climate of the learning environment
• Fostering and supporting positive behavior
• Teaching and fostering social skills
• Developing students' self-confidence and self-determination
• Encouraging the development of social and ethical principles
• Knowledge of pedagogy
• Establishing instructional goals
• Selecting appropriate materials and resources
• Partnering with colleagues, families, and the community as resources
• Designing and implementing instructional strategies
• Engaging students in reading and viewing a wide range of texts
• Providing instruction in processes, skills, and knowledge related to writing
• Equipping students to become effective communicators
• Developing students' appreciation for and capacity to use language
• Developing students' abilities to think mathematically
• Teaching inquiry
• Expanding the core curriculum to ensure the success of students with exceptional needs
• Evaluating student progress and making changes as necessary
• Creating and selecting diverse and valid assessment tools
• Differentiating instruction based on student strengths and needs
• Using assessment results to promote learning
• Providing feedback
• Collaborating to improve instruction and student learning (with families, colleagues, and the profession)
• Serving as links in family resource networks
• Advocating for students, subjects, and the profession
• Ensuring access to quality learning experiences
• Understanding how philosophical, historical, and legal foundations of the field inform effective practice
• Supporting student transitions and career development
• Managing time and human resources productively
• Engaging in reflective practices
	Content knowledge for each subject taught in the school, which may include the following:
	• American literature
	• Contemporary literature
	• Creative writing
	• Debate
	• English language and composition
	• Humanities
	• Journalism
	• Poetry
	• World literature
	• Algebra
	• Calculus
	• Geometry
	• Multivariable calculus
	• Probability
	• Statistics
	• Trigonometry
	• Biology
	• Chemistry
	• Earth science
	• Environmental studies
	• Physical science
	• Physics
	• Geography
	• International relations
	• Economics
	• Political studies
	• Psychology
	• Sociology
	• U.S. government
	• U.S. history
	• Women's studies
	• World history
	• Visual arts
	• Performing arts
	• Music
	• Physical education
	• Health
	• World languages, which may include but not be limited to
	  » American Sign Language
	  » Ancient Greek
	  » Arabic
	  » Chinese
	  » French
	  » German
	  » Hebrew
	  » Italian
	  » Japanese
	  » Korean
	  » Latin
	  » Portuguese
	  » Russian
	  » Spanish
	• Numerous electives

Source: Adapted from NBPTS Standards for Accomplished Teaching (EA-AYA/ELA, EA-AYA/Math and Exceptional Needs). Retrieved from http://www.nbpts.org/standards-five-core-propositions/.

It's unlikely, for example, that a high school principal—even one who has been a high school teacher—will have the expertise required to be an effective instructional leader with regard to every subject area, pedagogical practice, assessment strategy, student population, and special needs represented in a single high school.

The required expertise is not likely to exist in one individual, but it is likely to exist across a school. If we expand our thinking about what *leadership* means to include all who have expertise that could be a resource for improved teaching and learning, we begin to think beyond the principal and other formal members of school administration. We recognize the vast potential of teachers as leaders.

Leadership by All Teachers

From a distributed perspective, teachers are already leading in their schools. Leadership, at its core, is social influence (Chemers, 1997; Spillane, 2006), and teachers influence each other and each other's professional practice in many ways. They influence each other in formal and informal, intentional and unintentional, positive and negative ways. In this book, all of the ways teachers influence the quality of teaching and learning beyond their own classrooms are regarded as teacher leadership. In fact, their status as teachers enables them to have an influence throughout their schools.

Teachers' Leadership Influence

Teachers' influence on the quality of one another's teaching is obvious when a teacher is assigned to a role with a formal title or job description, or is supported with pay or release time to work in a role with a transparent objective that they pursue in a deliberate way (Berg & Zoellick, 2017). Such formal roles might include instructional coach, mentor, or leader of a professional development workshop. We tend to be less cognizant of informal ways in which teachers influence each other as they watch each other at work during a school assembly, motivate another to try a new strategy over lunch, share a resource at the copy machine, or engage in dialogue about student work on a bulletin board. From a distributed perspective, these informal interactions, when they are perceived as influencing the quality of one's teaching, are also potentially powerful forms of leadership (Spillane, 2006).

In fact, informal leadership is often quite unintentional. Recently a national board–certified teacher told me about one of his most powerful professional learning experiences. His student teacher looked around the classroom after the students had left for the day and asked, "Why is everything where it is?" They started at one end of the room and worked their way to the other, reflecting together on the position and layout of each main feature in their 2nd grade classroom and its impact on student learning, and—in the process—made significant improvements to the learning environment. The student teacher's probing question influenced this teacher in ways that had a powerful impact on student learning; thus, from a distributed perspective, the novice teacher's inquiry could be considered an act of leadership. What could be accomplished in a school where all teachers are in the habit of asking such probing questions?

Further, leadership can just as easily be experienced as negative instead of positive. We've all been part of a staff meeting where a new initiative is introduced. All it takes is one socially connected person to cross her arms and roll her eyes, and it is all over. The comments and body language of just a few can—intentionally or unintentionally—make or break the success of that initiative.

Unauthorized "stealth" teacher leadership is prevalent in schools, whether teachers are aware of it or not and whether principals would like to admit it or not. Leadership is occurring every time interactions affect the school's core work: student learning. The Leadership Tracking Tool in Figure 1.2 can help teacher/leaders note where stealth leadership may be happening in their schools. It does so by directing their gaze toward key leadership functions and who is behind them. From a distributed perspective, these are all leaders. Figure 1.2 presents this tool with sample responses. A blank copy is provided in Appendix A, as well as online.

FIGURE 1.2   LEADERSHIP TRACKING TOOL

Use the provided organizer to help you identify the interactions (tasks, activities, routines, etc.) that influence student learning in your school and the people who are involved.

Leadership Functions Necessary for Learning[1]	Interactions What tasks, activities, or routines occur in your school to influence this? In what ways is this being modeled, monitored, or advanced through dialogue?	People Involved Who are the people or teams involved in these interactions, in both intentional and unintentional ways?
School Learning Climate In what ways do our school's aims, values, and culture provide a focus on teaching and learning for students, teachers, administrators, and the wider community?	We revisit our core values and mission statement each year. We hold an assembly focused on one core value each month. We have a PBIS system. We communicate what we stand for and provide evidence of how we do that via our school website. We have shout-outs at the beginning of each faculty meeting.	Parent Council (leads core value and mission discussion each year) Faculty (has a voice in core value and mission revisions) Student Council advisor (directs Student Council in planning assemblies) Middle School Student Council (plans monthly school assemblies) PBIS Team (monitors PBIS system) School website webmaster (solicits content for website) Ms. Green (regularly offers shout-outs that focus on teaching and learning)

(continued)

FIGURE 1.2 LEADERSHIP TRACKING TOOL continued

Leadership Functions Necessary for Learning[1]	Interactions What tasks, activities, or routines occur in your school to influence this? In what ways is this being modeled, monitored, or advanced through dialogue?	People Involved Who are the people or teams involved in these interactions, in both intentional and unintentional ways?
Professional Capacity What ways does our school have for building individual and organizational knowledge about effective teaching and learning?	We have 40 hours of professional development (PD) throughout the year. Teachers who participate in PD beyond the school on release time are required to share their learning back at school. We have (voluntary) book clubs. We have subscriptions to professional literature in the teachers' room. We have mentors for every teacher with fewer than three years of experience.	Principal (sets priorities for PD; requires PD reports on external PD) Instructional Leadership Team (plans and evaluates PD; sometimes provides it) District departments (provide PD) Faculty (book club leaders and participants) School Parent Council (pays for book club books) Mr. Brown (leaves professional journals in the teachers' room) Mentor teachers
Shared Instructional Expectations In what ways do educators engage in dialogue that leads to shared expectations about teaching and learning and/or influences classroom practice?	At the start of each school year, we discuss shared expectations for instruction. We engage in looking at student work (LASW) at least four times per year in grade-level team meetings. We develop and collaboratively review common assessments. Each summer we review and adjust vertical curriculum maps for one content area. The district provides a list of sample "Look Fors" for each domain on the teacher evaluation rubric. Most teachers use the same lesson-planning template.	Principal (sets and communicates expectations) Grade-level team leaders (lead LASW) Teachers (bring work to LASW and/or contribute to conversation) Content leaders/department chairs (lead development of common assessments and curriculum mapping) District Dept. of Curriculum and Instruction (distributes Look Fors) Ms. Black (shared her lesson-planning template)
Family and Community Involvement In what ways does our school involve students, parents, and the wider community as partners in supporting student learning and their own learning?	We have an annual Math Night and a Literacy Night. We have a calendar of monthly family events. We have our Student Council produce monthly assemblies that demonstrate and reinforce our Core Values. We hold three-way conferences (student-parent-teacher) twice per year. We have university partners that provide student teaching and leadership interns. We have a monthly parent breakfast with the principal.	Math Department Leader (takes lead in organizing Math Night) ELA Department Leader (takes lead in organizing Literacy Night) Family Engagement Team (supports parent participation in all events) Student Council Advisor and members (Plan assemblies) Faculty (initiate parent conferences) University partners (assign interns; train mentor teachers) Ms. Blanco (attends parent breakfast to support communication with the principal, who doesn't speak Spanish)

FIGURE 1.2 LEADERSHIP TRACKING TOOL continued

Leadership Functions Necessary for Learning[1]	Interactions What tasks, activities, or routines occur in your school to influence this? In what ways is this being modeled, monitored, or advanced through dialogue?	People Involved Who are the people or teams involved in these interactions, in both intentional and unintentional ways?
Student Outcomes In what ways are we accountable for the impact of instruction on learning?	We share student work at three-way conferences with families. We make learning visible via assemblies, bulletin boards, and our website. We publish, share, and discuss our annual summative assessment scores. We use formative data to identify student learning gaps and adjust our teaching.	Students (choose student work to present at three-way conferences) Student Council (solicits assembly content) Faculty (determine content of their own bulletin boards) Webmaster (solicits website content) Principal (shares analysis of annual data results) Instructional Leadership Team (leads faculty discussion about annual data results) Grade-level team leaders (facilitate analysis of formative assessments and instructional responses to data) Ms. Burgundy (reminds us to disaggregate data and look at subgroup performance)
Other If we were to ask educators in our school to name the tasks, activities, and routines that have the most significant impact on the quality of the teaching and learning in their classrooms, what would they say? If they were not already captured above, add them here.	We have an annual opportunity to acquire new, high-quality instructional materials. We regularly revisit and revise our curriculum.	Principal (allocates budget allotment for new instructional materials) Mr. Grey (retired teacher returns as a volunteer to support curriculum development)

Examine the third column. These are all leaders.

- What patterns do you notice? What's missing?
- What was predictable to you? What surprised you?
- What do you wonder?
- What kind of small, strategic moves could increase the positive impact that formal and informal leaders are having in your school?

[1] School leadership encompasses responsibility for many aspects of schooling, from school operations to personnel management to program implementation. The leadership functions in this tool, adapted from *Organizing Schools for Improvement* (Bryk, Sebring, Allensworth, Easton, & Luppescu, 2010) and the National Center for School Leadership's model of learning-centered leadership (Southworth, 2005), encompass only the leadership functions that are most directly concerned with the quality of teaching and learning.

To be sure, principals have a significant measure of control over the conditions that support or limit teachers, parents, and students to be willing and able to interact and lead in these ways. These individuals and teams are performing leadership at the same time, whether they do so strategically and intentionally or organically and unintentionally. By reflecting on these interactions together, teacher/leaders can see a range of possibilities for increasing the impact of these formal and informal influences on student learning, and they can see a wealth of reasons why attention to co-performance among these many forms of leadership is needed.

Although much of the popular practice and literature on teacher leadership focuses on formalized leadership roles, this book takes a broader view: It seeks to maximize the ways in which *all* are leading in schools. From this perspective, teacher leadership is a culture change for all, not a special opportunity for a few. This perspective presents possibilities and challenges for schools.

Possibilities of Teacher Leadership

As teacher/leaders begin to recognize the many small ways in which classroom teachers are already influencing the quality of each other's teaching, it becomes useful to examine why and how this influence is possible. Doing so allows us to consider how teacher leadership might be tapped more deliberately as a strategy for greater student success.

Influence of teachers. One opportunity lies in understanding how teachers' influence is distinct from the influence of other leaders. Literature on teacher leadership points to a number of ways. First, teachers' work, occurring at the intersection where teaching and learning happen, gives them *grounded knowledge* that is unique to their position and is an asset when exerting influence (Elmore, 1990; Paulu & Winters, 1998). They know the students in front of them and are attuned—in a way other leaders are not—to the real place-based opportunities and challenges involved in trying to teach these students in this context. This gives teachers' leadership influence a unique brand of authenticity.

Second, teachers' *stance alongside their colleagues* is an asset. The traditional us-them dichotomy between teachers and administrators, which is often exacerbated by evaluation routines, tends to be absent in teacher leaders' relationships with their colleagues. To be sure, feelings of injustice or jealously over the assignment of limited formal roles can occur and relationships can still feel hierarchical among teachers. Yet researchers have found that having one foot in the classroom may give teachers more credibility and influence in pushing their colleagues' instructional practice than is the case for positional leaders like principals (Mangin & Stoelinga, 2008) and that working with colleagues can provide the boost of confidence and sense of self-efficacy that teachers need to take risks and improve their professional practice (Katzenmeyer &

Moller, 2009; Ovando, 1996). As they do so, they deepen relationships and lines of communication that support further change (Poekert, 2012). As members of the same "team," teachers may feel that teacher leaders are committed for the same reasons and that their actions will support or reflect poorly on all of them.

Finally, teachers tend to be *more accessible* to their colleagues than other leaders. They have more everyday opportunities to engage in the kind of casual, low-stakes conversations that build trust and are a necessary precursor to more challenging conversations that influence professional practice. In one study, teachers were more likely to approach each other informally than to approach formally designated teacher leaders (Supovitz, 2008); it seems accessibility matters, and it makes a difference for their learning. Teachers' close and frequent proximity to their colleagues allows teachers' professional learning to occur as close to practice as possible, which is seen as critical to truly changing teachers' practice (Frost, 2014; Fullan, 2007).

Influence on student learning. Another opportunity lies in thinking about the pathways through which teachers' leadership influence might have an influence on student learning. Although the progress of research on teacher leadership has been stymied by disagreement about what teacher leadership is (Mangin & Stoelinga, 2008; Wenner & Campbell, 2017), patterns can be found in the many ways researchers have traced a line—in theory or in practice—from teacher leadership to student learning. That is, teacher leaders can have an impact on student learning through their influence on teachers' expertise, school culture, or organizational improvement (see Figure 1.3).

Teachers can influence their colleagues' *expertise* in a variety of ways. They might do this, for example, from the vantage point of formal roles as mentors or instructional coaches, or by serving as professional learning leaders capable of increasing both the quantity and quality of professional development (Danielson, 2007; York-Barr & Duke, 2004). They might also exert influence in more subtle ways, because teachers tend to see their knowledgeable colleagues as resources regardless of whether or not they hold formal leadership roles (Margolis & Deuel, 2009; Spillane, Hopkins, Sweet, & Shirrell, 2017). Teaching is complex work involving a multitude of macro- and micro-decisions that require professional judgment. When teachers have the time and space for professional conversations with colleagues, they learn from each other's experiences and improve their decision making, regardless of any titles teachers may have (Danielson, 2015; Hargreaves & Fullan, 2012; McLaughlin & Talbert, 2001).

Teachers have also been found to influence *school culture* in ways that lead to school improvement. Engaging in teacher leadership can increase teachers' satisfaction and commitment (Johnson, Kraft, & Papay, 2012), which not only can set a tone throughout the school but also can affect their retention and result in

FIGURE 1.3 HOW TEACHER LEADERS INFLUENCE STUDENT LEARNING

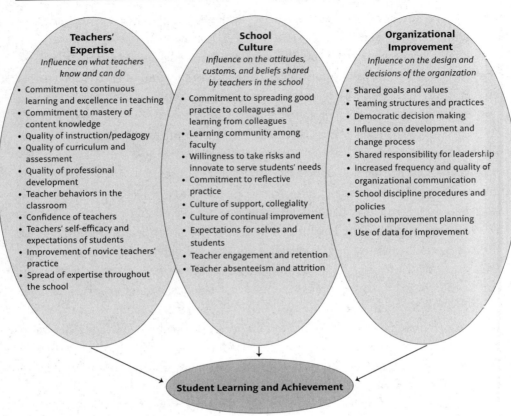

Teachers' Expertise
Influence on what teachers know and can do

- Commitment to continuous learning and excellence in teaching
- Commitment to mastery of content knowledge
- Quality of instruction/pedagogy
- Quality of curriculum and assessment
- Quality of professional development
- Teacher behaviors in the classroom
- Confidence of teachers
- Teachers' self-efficacy and expectations of students
- Improvement of novice teachers' practice
- Spread of expertise throughout the school

School Culture
Influence on the attitudes, customs, and beliefs shared by teachers in the school

- Commitment to spreading good practice to colleagues and learning from colleagues
- Learning community among faculty
- Willingness to take risks and innovate to serve students' needs
- Commitment to reflective practice
- Culture of support, collegiality
- Culture of continual improvement
- Expectations for selves and students
- Teacher engagement and retention
- Teacher absenteeism and attrition

Organizational Improvement
Influence on the design and decisions of the organization

- Shared goals and values
- Teaming structures and practices
- Democratic decision making
- Influence on development and change process
- Shared responsibility for leadership
- Increased frequency and quality of organizational communication
- School discipline procedures and policies
- School improvement planning
- Use of data for improvement

Student Learning and Achievement

Cautions:
1. These are potential influences. Teachers' leadership influence on these factors might be positive, neutral, or negative.
2. Context matters! Ask yourself: Under what conditions might teacher leadership result in this particular influence?

organizational stability that supports school improvement (Daly, Finnigan, & Liou, 2017; Johnson, Berg, & Donaldson, 2005). Teacher leadership can also improve morale and teachers' feelings of professionalism, both of which pay dividends in an increased sense of responsibility and collaboration (Harris & Muijs, 2004). Collaboration, for its part, has been found to have a systematic and positive effect on student learning outcomes (Ronfeldt, 2017; Togneri & Anderson, 2003). Some principals view this ability of teacher leaders to shape school culture as a real value. In one study, principals reported recruiting and growing national board–certified teachers with the deliberate intention of creating a climate more deeply committed to students' learning, reflective practice, and collaboration (Berg, 2007).

Teachers also influence the *organizational improvement* processes in their schools. They routinely engage in complex decision making in their own classrooms, but when they have a voice in schoolwide decision making, results are clear. They are able to bring their authentic, grounded classroom experiences to the table and contribute to better school procedures and planning processes (Ingersoll, Sirindes, & Dougherty, 2017; Little, 1990; Reynolds & Teddlie, 2000). In addition, in schools with teacher leadership, there can be improved implementation of new policies (Griffin, 1995), which may be due to a greater acceptance of school reform (Weiss & Cambone, 1994). Teacher leadership is helpful, and possibly even necessary, for strengthening schools as learning organizations (Silins & Mulford, 2004).

These opportunities point to important ways schools could tap in to teachers' individual passions, aspirations, and areas of expertise to elevate the quality of each other's work. It should be possible for teachers to be in the habit of influencing each other with challenging questions, exchanging expertise in ways that make all classrooms richer, and lending their informed voices to help shape the direction of the school. In these ways, each student in the school would be able to benefit from the collective expertise of the whole faculty, not just the teacher to whom they are assigned . . . in theory. In practice, this has proven a bit more difficult.

Challenges of Teacher Leadership

Until recently, teacher leadership development has largely been focused on the roles and capacity building of individuals, and not seen in context of the organizations in which teacher leaders work (Smylie & Denny, 1990). As a result, teachers who are otherwise prepared and trained to lead their colleagues frequently run into roadblocks. They encounter structural constraints, as they find they do not have the time they need, access to the information and people required, or the physical space to engage in formal or informal leadership roles. They often find that members throughout the organization are confused about the leadership role they hold: what it is, what authority it has, and how the role and its goals interact with other leadership roles or priorities (Bacharach, Bamberger, & Mitchell, 1990). In many schools, teacher leaders encounter professional norms that interfere with the notion of teachers influencing each other's instruction. Where teachers see feedback as intrusions on their autonomy, leadership roles as a threat to the egalitarian status quo, and seniority as more important than demonstrated expertise (Berg et al., 2005), they face a "triple threat" against teacher leadership that has persisted for decades (Johnson & Donaldson, 2007).

Principals have an essential role to play in addressing these structural, conceptual, and cultural barriers (Berg, Bosch, & Souvanna, 2013), but they can't do it alone. Teacher/leaders are all part of a system, and a change within one part of a system has repercussions throughout the system that teachers and principals do best to troubleshoot together. Where teachers in leadership roles have the principal's support in addressing these organizational issues, they are more effective (Leithwood, Seashore, Anderson, & Wahlstrom, 2004) and both teachers and principals are more satisfied (Datnow & Castellano, 2001; Marks & Nance, 2007).

Teacher Leadership Within a Leadership System

Getting all leaders—formal and informal, intentional and unintentional—on the same page is essential. Leadership is influence, and no one wants to be influenced in multiple directions at once. Thus, as we begin thinking about strategic support of teacher leadership, it's important to see teacher/leaders as part of a system.

When we take a distributed view and consider the wide range of stakeholders in a school that are perceived to influence teachers' professional practice, we see that the problem of incoherence could be considered inevitable. Although stakeholders tend to have the same general goals for students—21st century learning, college and career readiness, health and happiness—there is less agreement on what we will accept as evidence that we are meeting these goals. Reliable and timely data that are publicly acceptable and professionally credible for this purpose are elusive. Sources of data and evidence do exist, but the sources to which each stakeholder in the system has access (see Figure 1.4), and the meaning they make of them, vary.

FIGURE 1.4 STAKEHOLDERS AND THE EVIDENCE THEY HAVE ABOUT THE SYSTEM

Educators in the System	Evidence of School Success/Catalysts for Change
District and state administrators	State-, district-, and school-level data on student achievement (standardized test data only); political priorities; community input; teacher evaluation scores; educator retention data
School administrators: principals and assistant principals	School- and classroom-level data on student achievement, attendance, and behavior; climate surveys (teachers, families, students); classroom walkthroughs; teacher observation data
Classroom teachers	School-, classroom-, and individual-level data on student achievement; student intervention data; student work; observations of student engagement; conversations and observations about attendance and tardiness; family conferences; team conversations (e.g., looking at student work and collaborative planning)

From this perspective, it makes sense that teachers struggling to meet math goals would be angry about new district investments in a reading program, or that state administrators with a research-based plan for school turnaround cannot understand why district-level support seems to be lacking. None of these stakeholders has the whole picture.

Educators working within one system, yet looking at different forms of evidence from the vantage point of their own distinct roles and drawing different conclusions about a shared goal, could view this contrast of perspectives as a crisis, or they could work to make it an opportunity.

When committed educators at any level—classroom, school, district, or state—notice a gap between where they hope schools will be and what their evidence is suggesting, they get creative (Senge, 1990). The observation is a catalyst. They innervate and innovate. They think about what they can change. But they each have influence over different leverage points within the system. The Venn diagram in Figure 1.5 illustrates the kinds of changes that educators can make at different levels of leadership. The figure helps to highlight the unique and important contributions of each stakeholder, as well as the interconnectedness of those contributions.

FIGURE 1.5 POINTS OF LEVERAGE FOR IMPROVING THE QUALITY OF TEACHING, BY SYSTEM STAKEHOLDER

District and State Leaders

- Improve evaluation systems
- Influence quality of preparation programs
- Design and deliver professional learning opportunities
- Improve working conditions
- Support implementation of school improvement models
- Create incentives and recognition for quality teaching

- Establish and enforce policies and procedures that ensure school safety
- Engage in strategic planning
- Establish school goals and monitor benchmarks
- Make strategic decisions about the identification and allocation of resources

Principal Leaders

- Secure resources and establish priorities for school professional development (internal or external)
- Ensure time and space for collegial conversations and collaborative planning
- Hold teachers and self accountable for professional growth
- Be strategic about the number and selection of initiatives and partnerships

- Lead professional learning experiences
- Provide coaching with growth-oriented feedback
- Initiate informal conversations about instruction
- Establish and strengthen relational trust within the school
- Ask critical, probing questions
- Initiate a peer observation and feedback cycle
- Invite and engage voices of family and community in schoolwide decisions

Teacher Leaders*

- Identify personalized professional development (including articles, networks, courses, etc.)
- Engage in action research
- Invite colleagues to share insights and provide feedback
- Seek mentoring or modeling
- Reflect on own professional teaching practice

*Note: These points also apply to principal leaders and district and state leaders.

As we come to recognize that certain aspects of the system are visible only to select stakeholders—because of the evidence to which they have access for review—and that stakeholders can take only certain actions by virtue of their positions, we come to see the value and importance of working together. Each action taken by one stakeholder has implications for the others, so taking actions in sync is important. All of this requires the kind of attention to coordination that is not currently seen in most schools.

As a resident of Boston, I see this type of coordination quite frequently in a very different context. Few sights in Boston are as beautiful as the view of a crew team skimming along the Charles River at sunset. The coordinated effort of a crew team looks graceful and seamless . . . and easy. Crew team members will assure you it is not.

How do crew teams do it? Their success depends on being in sync. The angle of the oar and the shape of the stroke matter less than everyone's doing it together.

Crew teams work hard to develop a shared understanding about how their boat will look and feel when it is achieving peak performance. Such unity of vision enables each to make the decisions needed to do their part toward rowing in sync. If one member is eager to reach the finish line, she understands that rowing faster will not help.

CO-PERFORMANCE IN CREW; VIDEO ACTIVITY

WATCH: This short video—https://www.youtube.com/watch?v=YmoqjFRpu8A—features a college crew team discussing their co-performance.

EXTEND: What additional connections do you see between a crew team rowing a boat and and a school leadership team improving a school?

CRITIQUE: In what ways does this metaphor break down as a way of thinking about school improvement?

Crew team members also have a clear idea of the specific role each will play. Each seat in the boat has a different purpose and every member does not have to be good at every position. There's strategy, then, in matching each rower to an appropriate seat. Everyone is positioned to maximize their talents in service of the shared goal. And they have developed and practiced (and practiced and practiced) systems for communicating across their roles so that they can stay in perfect synchronization with one another as they go.

Finally, crew team members trust one another. They have faith that others will do their part and will work hard to be good at it, while showing respect and regard for teammates who are also trying their best. As they speed over the water in a direction they cannot see, they trust in the commitment of their peers and the call of the coxswain to synchronize their efforts and bring them safely and swiftly over the finish line.

These teams have something important to teach schools about co-performance of leadership. As educators open their eyes to the reality that teachers are already leading in powerful ways and open their minds to the many ways in which teachers have specialized expertise needed to transform schools, it becomes necessary to think about the practicalities of how best to tap into and align all of that capacity.

If we think of our school colleagues as a crew team, we recognize that we tend to share a general sense that the finish line has something to do with "student success," and spurred by an intense sense of urgency, we tend to hop into the boat wielding any kind of paddle, oar, or stick that we think is best and start splashing away. Such uncoordinated, well-intentioned actions inevitably counteract each other. We may find ourselves going nowhere, going in circles, or capsizing altogether. Even among faculty members with a shared agreement about the finish line and the ideal angle of our oars, we tend to overlook the need to keep track of how we're rowing, who should be seated where, and when we are rowing out of sync.

The subsequent chapters will help teacher/leaders learn together how to establish a shared vision for teaching and learning, develop routines to keep their efforts to pursue this vision in sync, and cultivate the trust needed to work and learn together.

Shared Vision

IN YOUR CONTEXT...

- What strategies do you use to clarify your own vision in your work?
- In what ways do colleagues communicate about their hopes for the work they share?
- What would it take to gain consensus around a shared vision for your shared work?

Leadership is about setting direction and leading others in that direction (Kotter, 1999). But when leadership is viewed from a distributed perspective, it reminds us to consider the following question: To what extent are formal and informal leaders in this context setting the *same* direction and leading others in that *same* direction? That doesn't happen without deliberate effort.

DAVIS ELEMENTARY SCHOOL

After 10 years as principal of Davis Elementary School, Principal Huff recognized a need for change. Test scores, which had been mediocre and stagnant, showed a slight dip in the past year and school culture had begun to show signs of decline, as evidenced by increased student discipline issues and staff turnover. Veteran staff members were going through the motions, and newer faculty who brought fresh ideas about teaching formed their own cliques.

Principal Huff started the school year with a passionate call to push for improvement. She displayed schoolwide data that showed how student achievement scores compared to district and state results. She shared research indicating that teaching is the most important school-based influence on student learning. And, modeling that she is a learner herself, she related key ideas from the summer leadership workshop she attended, emphasizing the importance of strong professional communities to school improvement. "This is the year we're going to work together to push and take this school to the next level!" she exhorted.

Teachers were genuinely energized by the idea that they would be supported to work together to achieve the kinds of successes with students that had motivated them to enter teaching in the first place. One thought, "We're finally going to embrace 21st century learning!" Another thought, "Now we can return to a focus on the whole child!" And still another thought, "At last we can get those test scores up!"

All educators want "student success," but each teacher/leader within a school may have a different idea of what student success looks like and how to achieve it. Although we often are unsure of the right way to go, we do know it is wrong to have everyone going in a different direction. This only serves to divert energy, dilute scarce resources, and set up a false and frustrating competition among leaders.

Having a shared vision of the goal is important for several reasons. A vision that is shared throughout a team motivates its members to take the risks needed to succeed and helps them feel responsible to each other as they strive toward the goal (Senge, 1990). It also binds members together through "moral purpose" and animates them to approach the work with ownership and creativity (Fullan, 2003).

Many schools initiate robust participatory efforts to create and revisit the school's mission and vision, but we don't always see such vision setting taking place for efforts that lie beneath the overall school purpose. What is the vision of this curricular change? This content team? This mentoring relationship?

When teacher/leaders take time to reflect upon the vision and purpose inspiring their work, and then work toward articulating a shared vision, the benefits are twofold. First, they develop shared understanding and ownership of the vision they have created, making it easier to align their efforts. Second, they become committed to doing it well and are empowered to design fresh approaches to reaching the goal.

For teacher/leaders to align their efforts and co-perform leadership effectively, they must spend time (1) clarifying their own vision of the goal, (2) improving communication about that goal, and (3) gaining consensus around a shared vision of what success will look like.

Clarifying One's Own Vision

Our vision is our high and worthwhile future hope for the work at hand. Our vision is our ideal. It is our definition of quality.

By the time we find ourselves working in a school, we have spent over 18,000 hours in classrooms as students ourselves, and we might feel we know good teaching when we see it. But, when push comes to shove, we're not always able to describe our vision of quality teaching. Further, each of us has spent those hours in different classrooms, and this affects our ability to talk to each other about it. We can benefit from some help in thinking about how to think about quality.

Considering Quality

When it was time to enroll my daughter in kindergarten, I joined a neighborhood group that had been formed by parents to help one another navigate Boston Public Schools' student assignment system, which at that time allowed parents to choose from dozens of schools. A lively discussion ensued as we shared what we were looking for in a school, and we explored the assumptions we had about quality teaching and learning. One parent was a university professor who wanted to see teachers implementing the latest research-based practices. Two parents argued that you can tell a school with quality teaching and learning simply by walking in the building and feeling the climate. Another claimed that entering the school was not necessary; quality teaching is evident by student learning outcomes. Personally, I wanted to know how teachers responded when students were stuck. Together we wondered which of these requirements for quality teaching were mutually exclusive. Which were necessary but not sufficient? Which were root causes, and which were potential outcomes of those causes? It was a rich discussion, and I found it ironic that I'd rarely had the opportunity to have a similar discussion with educators.

In many school contexts, the quality of teaching is a sticky conversation topic. Although teaching is uncertain work that requires myriad macro- and micro-decisions every hour, most educators find judgments about teachers' professional decision making hard to separate from judgments about the teacher who made those decisions. It's easier to write off the variations in teaching choices as differences in style, rather than to identify some decisions as higher-quality decisions than others. To be sure, making determinations about quality is subjective and challenging work, and stylistic variations make it all the more confounding. But, if educators want to improve teaching and learning, we need to be able to talk about how to increase the quality of teachers' decision making. We need to be clear about what problem we're solving—about the gap between the teaching or learning we have and the teaching or learning we want . . . and that students need.

An exercise to help us discover what we really think is to consider *what information we're using to make judgments about the quality of teaching*. If we can identify what is influencing our tacit judgments about teaching, then we can look together at those influences and start having more specific and effective conversations about our vision of high-quality teaching practice. Figure 2.1 identifies indicators we might inspect to make discernments about the quality of teaching and invites you to explore your own thinking about them.

The indicators presented in Figure 2.1 are quite varied. All are associated with quality teaching, but they each potentially reveal different kinds of information

FIGURE 2.1 FORMING OUR OWN JUDGMENTS ABOUT THE QUALITY OF TEACHING

Our discernments about the quality of teaching in a school or classroom are informed—consciously and subconsciously—by our observations about the quantity and quality of a variety of indicators, including some of those listed.

☐ Alumni cases	☐ Mission and vision
☐ Assessment practices	☐ Outreach to families and community
☐ Assignments/task demand	☐ Professional development
☐ Attendance of staff	☐ Progress monitoring of students
☐ Attendance of students	☐ Relationships: student-student
☐ Classroom culture and learning environment	☐ Relationships: teacher-student
☐ Classroom discussion/discourse	☐ Relationships: educator-educator
☐ Collaboration with colleagues	☐ Relationships: family engagement
☐ Communication routines	☐ Reputation in the community
☐ Curriculum implementation/fidelity	☐ School climate data
☐ Curriculum resources	☐ School climate plan
☐ Educators' content expertise	☐ Staff-to-student ratio
☐ Educators' years of experience	☐ Student behavior data
☐ Educators' reflective practice	☐ Student engagement
☐ Equity/attention to all students	☐ Student work samples
☐ Facilities (building and grounds)	☐ Teaming practices among educators
☐ Feedback to students	☐ Test scores (achievement or growth)
☐ Graduation retention of students	☐ Time for teaching and learning
☐ Instructional resources, including technology	☐ _____
☐ Instructional practices and strategies in use	☐ _____
☐ Intervention/reteaching systems	☐ _____

What influences your judgments about the quality of teaching?
1. Review the list above and check all that have an influence on your judgments about the quality of teaching practice. Add your own.
2. Identify your top five judgments and circle them. (Which five present the most convincing evidence to you that the quality of teaching is high?)
3. Consider the following questions:
   - Examine your top five priorities and explain why you have selected each. Why do you believe each is a more valid source of evidence than the nonranked choices?
   - How might awareness of the importance of these priorities to you affect your professional practice?
   - In your opinion, which are invalid indicators of quality teaching? Why?
   - How would/did your closest colleagues respond? (And what are the implications of the similarities and differences?)

about the quality of the system through which teaching causes learning. By teasing out these differences, we can distinguish for ourselves what contributes to quality, what is the result of quality, and what is required for quality from the work itself. We can clarify for ourselves our own role in creating quality.

Creating Quality

Some indicators refer to inputs to the education system. These are indicators that shape the context in which teaching and learning take place. Some inputs require a long-term investment or significant effort, for example, because they involve substantial resources or negotiation with others, and these might be categorized as *conditions*. Meanwhile, inputs that feel like they could be within educators' more immediate control as they make decisions within the given school year might be categorized simply as *determinations*. Labeling inputs as conditions or determinations is a subjective and context-dependent task. For example, in one district where decisions about curriculum resources are made annually at the district level, curriculum might be seen as a condition, whereas in another district curriculum might be a determination that teachers make. In addition, some items, such as professional development, might fall into multiple categories.

Other indicators refer to outcomes of the education system. Some are *outputs* that might be observable in students within the school year or immediately after it. Others are longer-term outcomes that could be considered *results* of the system.

Since teaching quality is the result of interconnected aspects of a large system, it's easy to confuse the inputs and outputs as well as the micro and macro ideas, and to end up with a notion that is too large or vague to be useful for improving the quality of teaching practice. Figure 2.2 invites you to collaborate with colleagues in teasing out the relationships of these indicators of quality (or other goals, if you adapt the questions) as you consider which part of the teaching and learning system each indicator may be exposing. Sample responses are included in the figure. A blank copy is provided in Appendix A, as well as online.

The reflection questions in Figure 2.2 shine a spotlight on the aspects of the system where educators have the most immediate control: the areas in which we are making determinations. Within the larger system that contributes to student and school success, quality involves making the best possible decisions about each of these indicators.

That said, clarifying one's own vision of quality *teaching* is particularly important because it is a prerequisite to being able to have productive conversations about improving teaching and learning together. All educators need practice in this area, because they cannot collaborate to improve teaching and learning if they cannot discuss teaching and learning and, more important, explain their discernments about quality in a detailed way.

FIGURE 2.2 INDICATORS OF QUALITY THROUGHOUT THE SYSTEM

Considering your context and the perspective of your current role, sort the *indicators* from Figure 2.1 into the columns below: Which are conditions? Determinations? Outputs? Results? In the process, if additional indicators occur to you, be sure to add those, too.

Conditions "of the context"	Determinations "of the educators"	Outputs "of the students"	Results "of the system"
Long-Term Inputs	*Short-Term Inputs*	*Short-Term Outcomes*	*Long-Term Outcomes*
Mission and vision School climate plan Facilities Instructional materials, including technology Curriculum resources Student data systems Time for teaching and learning Time for educator collaboration Professional development Staff ratio Educator years of experience Educator content expertise Decision making/ governance structure	School/classroom climate Curriculum implementation Instructional practices Assignments/task demand Feedback Progress monitoring Intervention/ reteaching Communication routines Teams Collaboration Outreach to families and community Relationships: • Educator-educator • Teacher-student • Family engagement Reputation in the community Professional development	Attendance Student engagement Student behavior School climate Student work • Completion • Quality • Quantity • Revision Relationships: • Student-student • Teacher-student • Family engagement Reputation in the community	Graduation/retention Academic achievement College-going rates Career pathways Alumni cases Reputation in the community

What is quality teaching?

Review your lists above and consider the following questions:

1. Are there any patterns? Any surprises? Where do your "top five" priorities fall?
2. What do you need to make strong decisions about each determination from Figure 2.1? What can/do you do to influence others to make stronger determinations?
3. How do your outputs relate to your determinations?
4. Take a critical look at the "Conditions" and "Determinations" columns: You placed indicators in the columns based on current policies and practices in your context. Are there any indicators you would move? That is, what do you believe *should* be up to teachers, individually and collectively?

Try using the indicators in the "Determinations" column to answer this question: What is quality teaching?

Communicating Our Way Toward a Shared Vision

Schools are places of improvement, yet simply imploring a school community to "improve" or exhorting a teacher to get "better" is far too vague to be useful. Improvement is change and it has a direction. What changes are we hoping to see? By when? And who says? When we remind ourselves that teacher/leaders throughout a school are already influencing each other's work, we begin to see the potential advantage in encouraging conversation about hopes, goals, quality, and vision among all those who share the work. Doing so can help the group shape its direction and stimulate more direct, intentional, and positive interaction among teachers. However, communicating about quality is not easy.

Communication Challenges

Even when we have our own vision of quality, we often struggle to communicate clearly with others about it. Back in my school choice parents group, the issue was glaring. There were too many school choices for any of us to visit all of them. One parent suggested that parents form pairs and triads to visit schools and report back. This was arranged and at the next meeting parents shared their assessments. Several parents had trouble going beyond statements such as, "It was such a great school!" or "It just gave me a bad feeling." Most found it hard to identify what gave them these feelings. When two parents were able to explain their choices, we were reminded of just how differently individuals can interpret the same situation. After these two parents visited the same school together, one parent reported: "Jefferson School had a great climate for teaching and learning: the students were lying all over the floor, boisterously working on projects in groups." Another parent described the same scene a bit differently: "Jefferson School had an awful climate for teaching and learning: the students were lying all over the floor, noisily distracting each other while out of their seats."

Teaching and learning are so complex that even the most expert among us may find ourselves tongue-tied. We don't necessarily have safe opportunities for practicing this conversation, but we can create them. Before doing so, however, we should consider why such conversations are so tricky.

One challenge educators face in communicating about quality is that it requires us to make our tacit knowledge explicit. We do what feels like the right thing to do at the time, but we rarely have time to think about why we do what we do, much less have time to practice articulating it. Even master teachers often can't explain what they do and why; they simply have a feel for what works. They are treasures for the students to whom they are assigned, but they cannot become the strong organizational assets their schools need them to be until they are able to engage in productive two-way conversations with colleagues that allow others to learn from the decisions they make in their professional practice. Some educators are simply at a loss for language and benefit from opportunities to practice putting what they do, and why, into words.

Another challenge is the imprecise language of education. Educators use terms in nuanced ways from team to team, school to school, and district to district.

Data-driven instruction? Some teachers are crunching numbers to look for gaps that must be addressed; others are examining portfolios of student work samples to understand how students have been approaching their work. Student-centered learning? For some this conjures images of students learning cooperatively, while others are thinking about individual personalized instruction on a computer. We frequently use acronyms that may be unknown to others or carry slightly different meaning across contexts. PLC, COP, PLN, ILT, SST, RTI, SEL, LEP. . . . Even if one is able to determine what the acronyms stand for, the meaning and use of the term may vary. Does *CPT* refer to a time of day (common planning time, when prep periods are aligned), a team of people ("My CPT discussed common assessments today"), or a type of meeting (any in which teachers are planning together)? Through use, words take on a shared meaning and colleagues develop a shared vocabulary.

Finally, there is an emotional factor. The term *teacher* doesn't describe a job we have; it is who we are. We internalize the work and define ourselves by it. Teaching can feel very personal, and a discussion about differences in the quality of teaching practice (or other aspects of our practice, such as curricular adoption, our teaming, or our mentoring relationships) can feel like a personal assault. In fact, communicating one's own vision out loud and to others may feel risky to some. What if others don't agree? The idea of working toward a shared vision is even riskier. Might I have to give up some principles I hold dear? Most educators will not be willing to fully engage in that conversation unless they trust their colleagues. Trust is a critical foundation for this work. In Chapter 5, I discuss trust further, including how it is established and what teacher/leaders can do to strengthen it.

Confidence Through Conversation

Confidence can be gained through conversation, as teacher/leaders become accustomed to viewing and responding to each other's work. Figure 2.3 offers some ideas about how educators, whether teacher/leaders with informal influence or those with formal authority, might capitalize on existing interactions as opportunities to initiate deliberate conversations about quality teaching. One could imagine how these same ideas could be adapted to help open dialogue about quality in other areas of work, from curriculum implementation (e.g., sharing and discussing public videos, bulletin boards, or teachers' stories about implementing the curriculum), to team meetings (e.g., building in meeting routines to examine the impact of our work, reflecting on how key meeting situations were handled, or sharing bright spots), to mentoring relationships (e.g., collaborating to document and discuss what is working well, reflecting together on the impact of the mentoring conversations, or keeping a list of routines that are worth sharing with other school

FIGURE 2.3 STIMULATING CONVERSATIONS ABOUT THE QUALITY OF TEACHING

Everyone can turn everyday interactions into valuable opportunities to practice conversations about quality and build trust.

	Professional Interactions	Informal Leaders	Formal Leaders
Lower-stakes interactions: a view into colleagues' work	**Anonymous performances** (e.g., videos from the web, visiting another school, unidentified student work samples)	Establish a social media group (e.g., Twitter, Google Group, or Slack) through which teachers can share classroom photos, videos, and student work and commentary on why they have shared it	Share anonymous performances within staff meetings or professional development; facilitate critical conversations about the quality of them
	Public performances (e.g., bulletin boards, assembly performances)	Collaborate to create bulletin boards or assembly performances and initiate conversations about the quality of the work on display	Organize a bulletin board or classroom scavenger hunt: Look for good ideas on your colleagues' walls, then come back and share what made them good
	Meetings (e.g., team/staff meetings, workshops)	Ask critical questions that bring the conversation back to the impact on student learning	Build classroom sharing into meeting routines: powerful teaching moment of the week, and so on
	Curated performances (e.g., selected student work, video-recorded lessons)	*Ask a colleague to share some student responses to an assignment you created together *Seek colleagues' advice in response to student performances that puzzle you	Protect time in meeting agendas for looking together at student work
	Accidental observation (e.g., during co-teaching, hallway interactions)	Solicit feedback on your practice or how you handled a given situation from a colleague who teaches in your room or has witnessed your interactions with students	Encourage teachers who work in each other's classrooms to speak up about bright spots, pose questions, and share reflections
	Deliberate observation (e.g., peer observation, walk-throughs)	Propose inter-classroom visits with a colleague, then be sure to conference about the visits afterward	Support the development of a peer-observation and/or walk-through routine to include all instructional staff
Higher-stakes interactions: a view of colleagues at work	**Educating each other** (e.g., mentoring, leading professional development)	*Organize an Edcamp *Reach out to new colleagues with offers of support to help them learn and meet school expectations for quality instruction	Create the expectation and time for teachers to share with school colleagues learning from external professional learning experiences

colleagues). Over time, as shared language is established and trust is built, conversations can evolve from safe (finding points of agreement) to healthy high-risk (debating divergent views). It's the latter conversations that move a school forward.

The more educators have opportunities to talk with each other about instruction and to practice explaining to one another how they make determinations within their teaching, the better they will become at communicating about and comprehending what each other means by *quality teaching*.

But, that doesn't mean they will agree.

Aligning in a Shared Vision

Once teachers/leaders articulate their conceptions of quality and engage in conversation, they are able to take the next critical step: getting in sync through a *shared* vision. Is this a tango, a waltz, or a square dance? Let's not assume all know which dance we're doing. Explicit agreement is necessary so that we can not only avoid stepping on each other's toes but also maximize our impact with coordinated moves.

The needs in schools are urgent and resources in schools are scarce—most notably educators' time—so teacher/leaders need to be efficient and effective. Having each individual pursue their own vision leads to incoherence, no matter how lofty each educator's goals. Without attention to a shared vision, there is wasted effort, something schools cannot afford.

False Alignment

Everyone shares a vision that novice teachers will become able to practice high-quality teaching. However, the conception of quality teaching laid out in a teacher preparation program rarely aligns with the professional practice of a supervising teacher. Licensure requirements communicate a third conception of quality teaching. A new teacher is recruited to a district by materials that make claims about what teaching is like there. Yet, once settled in a school, the novice finds the principal may have their own nuanced expectations of good teaching. While struggling in the first year to make sense of these varied conceptions, the novice teacher is then "supported" by a mentor who may come in with their own ideas about good teaching and be evaluated according to an evaluation framework that may or may not be aligned with any of the previous conceptions. In this extreme, but not necessarily atypical example, one could easily imagine that the quality of the novice teacher's instruction (as well as the teacher's sanity) might actually decline with all this "help." The novice would be better supported if these varied influences—mentors, supervisors, and colleagues—were aligned, if they took time to choreograph their moves and work in sync.

Each stakeholder in this illustration has a clear vision. Each has clearly communicated that vision. The preparation program has "Ten Principles for Educator Effectiveness," the state has "Four Standards for Professional Licensure," the district has "Eight Dimensions of Effective Teaching," the school principal has "Seven Habits of Excellent Educators," and the mentor teacher has their own list of dos and don'ts. It is as though these coaches are preparing the novice for a dance performance without first agreeing on the song.

Beneath the language, to be sure, there are some core concepts in common. We could pick one vision and align the others to it. But which one? And what do we do about the areas in which they don't align? Are there good ideas we all can adopt? If educators can agree on an aligned conception of quality teaching and learning, their individual efforts to influence it can have greater collective impact. And, most important, each member can think about how their own unique skills can contribute to co-performance of the work.

Try the activity in Figure 2.4 with a team of colleagues and reflect on your experience using the questions provided. Teams that take on this activity find different approaches to achieving the unity of vision and action needed to complete

FIGURE 2.4 SYNC OR FLOAT

Invite your team to take on the following challenge. All you need is a long stick, such as a broom handle.

Instructions
1. Invite the team to form two lines facing each other and ask members to extend one hand into the space between these lines with palm up and one index finger out.
2. Explain that you will place the broomstick on their outstretched fingers. All they have to do is lower the stick to the floor, while following two simple rules:
   - The stick must rest on top of their fingers.
   - Everyone's finger must remain touching the stick at all times.
3. Lay the stick on their fingers, and stand at the end of the line to monitor the rules.
4. Go!

Debrief Questions
After the first failure:
- Did everyone understand the goal? And the rules?

After the second failure:
- Is anyone doing this on purpose? Sabotaging the effort? Does everyone want to succeed here?

After success:
- What went wrong at first (with our process)? What was the problem?
- What happened when we didn't succeed? What did you see and hear? What did you feel? (Be real: There may be blame, giving up, teasing, etc.)
- What helped us succeed?
- What happened when we did succeed? What did you see and hear? And feel?
- Have you ever been a part of other efforts in which everyone was well-intentioned but unable to succeed?
- What does it take to support members to sync their efforts and reach a goal?

What happens? [Spoiler Alert!]
- As members try to remain in contact with the stick, they inadvertently push upward and the stick rises up in the air.
- With some discussion and patience, they can do it. This requires everyone's effort, but more important, it requires everyone to coordinate their efforts.

Facilitator tip: When placing the stick, before you let go, press down a bit to ensure that members feel the need to compensate!

the task. Each member begins with their own idea of what needs to happen, which leads to collective failure, and eventually members come to a shared understanding that allows them to succeed. What happens? There is not one common path to unity of vision, though in this activity, as in life, it often gets a bit ugly before it gets pretty.

Teacher/leaders can help their colleagues persevere and come to a shared vision when they remind them to do two things: draw on diverse perspectives and keep students at the center.

Drawing on Diverse Perspectives

When we recognize the value in our diverse perspectives, we believe that what we can create together is genuinely better than what we could have accomplished alone. The conversations that bring us closer to consensus will be challenging, but the effort will be worth it, as these conversations allow different perspectives to surface and enrich our collective thinking.

Today, in some contexts, a principal or superintendent is the chief arbiter of what good teaching is. In other contexts, parents and student opinion have a lot of sway in the locally accepted conception of quality teaching. Alternatively, the decision may lie beyond individuals. Instead, evaluation tools or student assessment results set the boundaries on what good teaching is and is not. Each of these influences comes from a particular viewpoint and is grounded in a reason worth considering in discussion.

Too often when there are differences of opinion, we compare them all and accept the few that everyone can agree with. In our avoidance of true dialogue and potential confrontation, we end up with a compromise that represents the lowest common denominator, instead of a solution that benefits from the rich exchange of ideas.

It is each teacher/leader's responsibility to guard against this and to ensure that the group is truly maximizing the expertise and experience of all, enabling each to influence one another in direct, intentional, positive ways.

Decisions about quality are happening at every level of leadership, and many factors contribute to who makes these decisions and how. State-level decisions about quality schools may be necessary to inverve in schools that are not providing sufficient opportunities to learn. School-level decisions about the school's overall vision benefit from the positional authority of the principal, which gives the community confidence that they will be supported and held accountable to that vision. Ultimately, those decisions lead to better outcomes when decision-makers are able to engage the community in that vision-setting process in a meaningful way.

Decisions about the vision of quality benefit from the fresh thinking of multiple stakeholders who may be affect by the decisions being made: What are the goals for our new curriculum implementation? What's the vision of our content team? What do we value about mentoring relationships? There are different perspectives, and our differences matter. Figure 2.5 describes an activity to use with colleagues to help them consider how difference matters.

FIGURE 2.5 DIVERSITY ROUNDS

How might knowing the actual country of origin of first-generation students, the home language, the birth order, or the perceived strengths of our students influence teaching and learning? Explore why it matters.

In this activity, participants will be forming and reforming groups of different sizes. They will need sufficient space to stand and move around. The activity requires 30–60 minutes.

1. Explain to participants that they will be asked to form groups according to different categories and will have five minutes for discussion within these groups. The categories are open to interpretation; participants are to define them with others as they form groups.

2. Ask participants to form groups by "birth order." Ask them to discuss the posted questions for five minutes, and alert them that they will report them back briefly at the end:
   a. What does it mean to you to be _____? How much do you define yourself this way?
   b. How is our group unique/different from other groups?
   c. One thing we would like other groups to know about us is _____.
   d. How does being _____ affect my experience as an educator?

3. Ask each group to report out, focusing primarily on questions c and d.
   How does it feel to have that label?
   Did anyone have to reframe themselves to fit a group? How did that feel?

4. Repeat with a total of three to five categories, selecting them based on what makes sense in your context. Some options are
   Birthplace
   Home language
   Something you're good at
   Role in school
   Years in this school

5. Lead a reflective conversation about the activity:
   How did you feel about doing this exercise? Did your feelings change from the first to last round?
   What did it bring up that was new for you?
   What was difficult? Uncomfortable? Comforting?
   What observations did you have about how groups came to be defined?
   Would you use this activity with others?

Source: Adapted from School Reform Initiative. (n.d.). *Diversity rounds.* Retrieved from http://schoolreforminitiative.org/doc/diversity_rounds.pdf

Keeping Students at the Center

In fact, our students are all different and their differences matter, too. Since the purpose of teaching and schooling is student growth, and since students vary as individuals and as populations, it makes sense to put students at the center of our vision-setting conversations. Learning targets that are essential in one context might be viewed with less urgency in another. "Best practices" that work in one context may not work in another. Context matters. It is worth taking time to understand what is unique and important about the specific collection of individual students in our care, what they need to learn, and how they will best learn it. Students must be at the center because teaching that is not helping students meet important goals is not quality teaching. To approach a shared vision of quality that has students at the center, it is important to know who those students are.

To achieve unity of vision, then, educators need to share a clear, compelling picture of the goal. They need to know what, specifically, will be different, and in fact better, that will make the difficult conversation worth it. It allows them to keep their eyes on the prize and to feel encouraged as they approach it.

A first step for teacher/leaders to achieve this unity of vision is to look together at student data. This allows them to establish a common, evidence-based understanding of what specific problem(s) they are solving before they seek solutions (and then decide) on a unified course of action.

We need to know who our students are as groups and as individuals before we consider the implications for our expectations of quality teaching. Computer literacy might be valued, but we don't want to assign homework that requires Internet access if we know that few students in the community have access to it. "Best practice" tells us that students need feedback. Our knowledge of students should inform our decisions in determining the frequency, language, and delivery method for feedback that will have the greatest impact.

In 2014, a study examining culturally relevant practices in the Boston Public Schools identified a school with a significant Latino population (35 percent) in which the only cultural displays or curricular connection to Latin culture was an annual Cinco de Mayo celebration, yet none of the Latino students were Mexican (Miranda et al., 2014, pp. 60–61). Culture studies of Cinco de Mayo can be valuable for all students, yet schools with limited resources might maximize their impact by thinking strategically about their own specific student populations and the most high-leverage ways to employ those resources so that students have meaningful teaching and learning experiences. If quality teaching is the goal, we can't get away without truly knowing our students.

Today, teachers have access to a variety of sources of information that can provide them with a rich picture of students' backgrounds, experiences, strengths, and assets. Most schools have data systems that can provide statistics on demographics and historical data on student performance. Effective teachers collect their own data as well, for example, by conducting observations, home visits, parent conferences, or student interviews. There is tremendous value, however, in making these practices teamwide or schoolwide routines and taking time to talk about the results. By looking at multiple data sources together (see Figure 2.6), educators can make more well-informed teamwide or schoolwide decisions, such as determinations about curriculum investments, professional development, scheduling,

FIGURE 2.6 MULTIPLE DATA SOURCES

People	*Demographic data:* age, ZIP code, race/ethnicity, ELL status/home language, special education code, free and reduced-price lunch program (FRLP) status, parent education, and so on.
Perceptions	*Survey/interview data:* What do students and family members perceive as student strengths, challenges, and opportunities? School strengths, challenges, and opportunities? What are potential threats to success?
Practices	*Observation data:* What are students doing? What are the students' behaviors, social skills, learning styles, and work habits like?
Performance	*Student achievement data:* summative and formative academic performance data, grades, student work, personal achievements in sports, arts, and so on.

Adapted from Bernhardt, 1998, p. 6.

programming, and family engagement efforts. More important, the conversations that educators have as they compile and analyze these data across classrooms leads to the development of shared understanding of who our students are and a common language for discussing their needs, both of which help establish a critical foundation for developing a shared vision of quality teaching in our schools.

After looking at data, it's worth revisiting your work from Figure 2.2 with your own students in mind. The sample figure is reprinted in Figure 2.7 with new reflection questions. This time we note that the second two columns are really asking, "What do our students need? (What outcomes are important?)" Meanwhile, the first two columns are asking, "What do our students need *from us*? (What inputs will result in those outcomes?)" You can use your knowledge of your students to review the inputs and prioritize them with your colleagues. Add adjectives and qualifiers. Collapse and categorize them. Together with your team, you can develop a paragraph, perhaps even a catchy acronym, that highlights shared beliefs about good teaching in your context. A blank copy is provided in Appendix A, as well as online.

Wrestling with these questions can help teams to develop common understandings and gain consensus on the vision of quality teaching. How might this conversation happen? A lot of indicators could be addressed. A principal might provide clarification on some, opening up only a few for discussion at one time. A leadership team might take them all on together in a retreat setting. A full faculty could engage with a few indicators each month through the use of online polling tools or a gamelike structure in a staff meeting, for example, by asking, "What does high-quality [indicator] look like?" Then the faculty would review the range of responses for that indicator.

The process is as important as the product because the dialogue process leads to shared meaning. Ideally, all who have the potential to exert leadership influence have a place in the conversation (see the accompanying example from

FIGURE 2.7 INDICATORS OF QUALITY (REPRISE)

What do our students need from us? (What factors will contribute to desired outcomes?) *What is high-quality teaching?*		What do our students need? (What results are important?) *What is high-quality learning?*	
Conditions	**Inputs**	**Outputs**	**Outcomes**
Long-Term Inputs	*Short-Term Inputs*	*Short-Term Outcomes*	*Long-Term Outcomes*
Mission and vision Facilities Instructional materials, including technology Curriculum resources Student data systems Time for teaching and learning Time for educator collaboration Professional development Staff ratio Educator years of experience Educator content knowledge Decision-making/governance structure	School/classroom climate Curriculum implementation Instructional practices Assignments/task demand Feedback Progress monitoring Intervention/reteaching Communication routines Teams Collaboration Outreach to families and community Relationships: • Educator-educator • Teacher-student • Family engagement Reputation in the community	Attendance Student engagement Student behavior School climate Student work • Completion • Quality • Quantity • Revision Relationships: • Student-student • Teacher-student • Family engagement Reputation in the community	Graduation/retention Academic achievement College-going rates Career pathways Alumni cases Reputation in the community

Consider these questions together with your colleagues or leadership team:

1. *Indicators of quality:* What are our assumptions about what each looks like at a high level? What are the implications for students if we have multiple (formal and informal) leaders with different assumptions?
2. *Knowledge of students:* How does our knowledge of students affect our determinations about the quality of these indicators? About priorities?
3. *Underlying values:* Ultimately, our assumptions derive from underlying values that we hold. Together, can we identify them?
4. *Work toward agreement:* What expectations can we agree upon? Add adjectives, quantities, and qualifiers before each indicator.
5. *Identify and agree upon priorities:* Which indicators are most important for these students? Which should we focus on first?
6. *Consider the nested system:* Schools are nested within districts, and districts within states. Schools inherit the priorities and mission statements of the systems in which they reside. What important part does our school play in the district's mission? How does our vision of quality teaching align with the district's mission?

Massachusetts). Through conversation, educators build understanding, trust, and shared language, which are critical to the next steps.

As the conversations continue, educators develop an ever-clearer understanding of the kind of high-quality teaching expected in this context, and they can better support each other to practice it. Just how they support it, the roles each plays, and how to coordinate their efforts is the subject of the next chapter.

A COMMON, SHARED VISION: MASSACHUSETTS

In 1990, the Massachusetts Department of Education initiated a statewide dialogue about learning outcomes. Citizens were asked, "What is your idea of a well-educated Massachusetts high school graduate?" More than 50,000 Massachusetts residents—students, parents, educators, school partners, higher education faculty, business community members, policymakers, and others—weighed in by letter, phone, and forums held throughout the state, the results of which were aggregated and used to define the *Common Core of Learning*. This document declares, "The goals reflect what citizens highly value and see as essential for success in our democratic society." The document was then used to "provide a focus for improving education in the Commonwealth," as it became the backbone of our state's first set of Curriculum Frameworks and related comprehensive assessment system. It was a cumbersome and time-consuming process, to be sure, but the statewide engagement in the process and the rich discussions about what we really believe is important about schooling were valuable for achieving a vivid picture of our shared vision and common language with which to continue conversations about making that vision a reality.

Source: Berg (2010); Commonwealth of Massachusetts (1994).

A RETURN TO DAVIS ELEMENTARY SCHOOL

Principal Huff had promised her staff, "This is the year we're going to work together to push and take this school to the next level." Her faculty, however, had divergent opinions on what that next level might look like, and strong reasons behind each.

Principal Huff recognized the enthusiasm of the faculty and the cordial relationships among them as assets on which she could build. She reflected that each member of her faculty had important strengths that were unknown to their colleagues and could be a part of the solution. But, instead of jumping to solutions, which might have divided the staff into teams pitting their favorite ideas against each other, she engaged the faculty in further definition of the problem.

She followed her presentation of schoolwide data with opportunities for grade-level teams to engage more deeply in understanding who their students were and what they needed (see Figure 2.6) through interviews with students, conferences with parents, and looking together at various student learning artifacts and data. Representatives of those teams brought their teams' learning to the schoolwide instructional leadership team that used this information to think critically about which indicators of quality in their system (see Figure 2.1) might be most relevant and important for these students at this time, and which long- and short-term inputs might be a worthwhile focus of special attention in the year ahead (see

Figure 2.2). The conversation spilled over into other formal meetings in the school and into informal interactions (see Figure 2.3), which served to deepen everyone's thinking about what quality teaching and learning should look like for the students they share. Next, understanding the benefits of a unified course of action (see Figure 2.4), as well as the value of the diverse perspectives on the team (see Figure 2.5), they revisited the indicators of quality conversation (see Figure 2.7) and ironed out agreements about a new schoolwide vision for high-quality teaching, one around which they could choreograph their efforts and stay in sync.

Reflection

1. Review your responses to the context questions at the beginning of this chapter. What new reflections do you have, and what possibilities for action do you see?
2. How might the ideas and strategies from this chapter help teacher/leaders in your school to co-perform leadership more skillfully?

Leadership Co-Performance

IN YOUR CONTEXT . . .

- How is teacher/leaders' influence aligned with your school's key leadership functions and priorities? And with each other?
- To what extent are you aware of the expertise teacher/leaders have that could be an asset for those leadership functions and priorities?
- What leadership knowledge and skills do teacher/leaders need to develop, and what opportunities do they have to do so together?

Teacher/leaders with a shared vision have the foundation needed for partnership in improvement, yet this is not enough because there are many potential pathways to achieving that vision. Some of those paths will be complementary and mutually supportive. Others will compete for scarce resources, result in duplication of efforts, or create confusion. If we aim to maximize the potential leadership influence of all teacher/leaders toward this vision, then we need to think strategically about how they will co-perform leadership functions. We should think about what needs to be done, who should be doing it, and how they might be supported to do it well.

PEARL MIDDLE SCHOOL

The staff of Pearl Middle School made a unified commitment to personalized learning. They listened to an inspirational speaker on the topic, heard positive stories from other schools that had made this shift, and engaged community members in the discussion about how and why next year would be different.

That summer, teacher/leaders got going: Members of the 8th grade team used their district-provided professional development (PD) stipends to take a year-long graduate course together, the principal allocated the bulk of the funds in her PD budget to purchase multiple copies of a book on personalized learning and to bring in the author to speak to the faculty, the literacy coach designed some after-school PD sessions, the technology liaison began setting up a Google Classroom that teachers could use to manage shared information and resources, and the 7th grade team succeeded in its GoFundMe campaign to purchase a Chromebook cart to support the use of online learning tools. They all returned to school in the fall feeling excited and ready to dive into personalized learning.

When the school year began, the literacy coach shared a schedule of after-school PD, but the dates conflicted with the dates for the graduate course that the 8th grade team would continue taking through the year. The 8th grade team members returned excited to teach their colleagues about the strategies for managing personalized learning that they picked up during their summer learning, until they discovered that the tech liaison's Google Classroom duplicated some of that effort. The tech liaison also identified online reading and resources for the faculty to explore so that they could develop shared language and have a "touchstone text," though the principal had already invested in a different text. The text had a useful list of recommended apps, many of which were not compatible with the new Chromebooks.

Under what conditions might this flurry of well-intentioned effort lead to improvement (see Figure 3.1)? All are committed to personalized learning. In this case, they even have a shared vision of the personalized learning they want to see for students. But they have not taken time to coordinate their actions and synchronize their efforts. They need to work out their dance routine. This situation requires attention to co-performance.

FIGURE 3.1 COMMITMENT TO PERSONALIZED LEARNING

Commitment to Personalized Learning

?

Personalized Learning for All Students

Whether a faculty has decided on a curricular approach, a department has committed together to developing new assessments, or a team is planning a school assembly, getting a community to share the same vision for what they plan to accomplish is only the beginning of the work. This is because there are many beliefs and opinions about the best way to achieve a vision, and it is counter-productive to implement all of them at once. Schools are systems and they have limited resources, so it's important to consider the net effect of the people and policies working within it, not just the merit of each individual's approach. With recognition that all are potentially exerting a leadership influence, how do we increase the likelihood that teacher/leaders' influence is positive and aligned with a shared vision?

Research suggests that attention to leaders' co-performance is worthwhile. Researchers have long documented patterns in shared leadership (Pearce & Conger, 2003), but only recently have they looked closely at the impacts of organizing schools to deliberately maximize the multiple sources of leadership. They find, for example, that such schools benefit from access to a greater range of knowledge and experience, which not only has direct benefit to the organization but also increases opportunities for members to learn from each other. In addition, in deliberately distributed leadership systems, teachers feel empowered to participate in decision making, have a better sense of the organization's needs, and are more attuned to how their own behavior influences others (Gronn, 2002). Though studies have documented patterns in the distribution of leadership and the various ways of co-performing leadership functions (Spillane, 2006), there are no research-based conclusions about the best ways to do so (Louis et al., 2010). Teacher/leaders need to work out their own dance steps together. This chapter presents a series of tools designed to help.

Co-Performance of Leadership Functions

Teacher/leaders might start by considering together the leadership functions that are essential in their school. This will allow them to think critically about the ways teacher/leaders are already co-performing leadership and to think creatively about how they could improve their co-performance of these functions.

Functions Before Form

I recently went to a potluck dinner and brought a salad. When I arrived, I noticed that nearly everyone had brought salad. We all knew we were coming to celebrate a friend who is fond of healthy food, so we had the same vision of the end goal: to honor her with a meal she would like. But since we didn't talk about how we might reach that goal in a way that would produce a balanced meal, there was duplication of efforts (and way too much kale—ugh!).

This is a simple problem with low stakes, and I don't think the guest of honor felt any less celebrated by our redundant contributions. School improvement, by contrast, is complex work that carries high stakes. It cannot be accomplished through potluck contributions, no matter how well intentioned.

To be sure, schools have simple problems, too. Time to put on an assembly? We'll divide up the tasks and get it done. But close the achievement gap? Adopt project-based learning? Rescue the school from the brink of state takeover? For these problems we need to think about the functions that are essential for accomplishing the goal, not simply what form each person's role will take. This is because the work is too complex. There will be unforeseen variables and constant change, and the system will need to be able to respond. When the players know each other's functions and how they relate, they can better predict how the system will shift in the face of change. If we don't simply assign roles, but instead agree together about key functions that need to be filled, then when there is a change we'll be able to make midcourse corrections that are appropriate and predictable.

In the potluck example, what key functions need to be filled? After we get on the same page about what a "good meal" looks like (see Chapter 2), we can work together to articulate the key components of a good meal. Which courses are required? Whether these components are defined by one individual, by a team, or through engagement of the whole group, they provide the structure needed for coordinated co-performance: Participants will have the information they need to make decisions that work for them and that are aligned to the group. That is, the categories allow individuals to have some choice over what they bring, while ensuring that the parts will come together in a satisfying whole. And, in the end, the meal is better than any an individual could have pulled together alone. Attendees with an abundance of garden tomatoes can bring a dish that highlights those, while those who are skilled at making desserts can choose to specialize there. The beauty is that, with just a little bit of forethought about the functions that must be co-performed, (1) everyone doesn't have to bring everything, and (2) everyone can bring what best suits their skills and abilities.

The teams we form in schools are rarely composed with such deliberate thought, and the roles we play are often defined by tradition and assigned based on who is available. One might retort that there is not enough flexibility in the schedule or faculty to strategically staff a team. I would counter that if the team's work is important, it should be composed with—or supported to grow—the expertise needed to fulfill its core functions. If the team's work isn't important, then why is it meeting in the first place?

Mapping Leadership Functions

Principals often talk about keeping all the balls in the air. But what are the balls, as they see them? How many of them are there? If we can define them, we might be able to engage in a "team juggle." It helps to have shared language.

The leadership literature takes many approaches to breaking down leadership into its component parts. There are lists of *what leaders need to know,* including national and state standards for school administrators and, in some locales, for teacher leaders. There are lists of *what leaders do,* such as Sergiovanni's (1984) "Five Leadership Forces" or the much more specific "21 Responsibilities of the School Leader" from Marzano, Waters, & McNulty (2005). Numerous *leadership styles* (see, for example, Evans & Teddlie, 1995; High & Achilles, 1986) have also been articulated in the literature. None of these is nearly as useful for thinking about the co-performance of leadership as is a list of *leadership functions,* because they do not describe what has to be accomplished. By focusing on functions, teacher/leaders are free to move beyond existing conceptions of what leaders need to know, do, and be like. They can consider new ways to accomplish those functions.

One research-based framework for thinking about leadership functions has been put forward by the University of Chicago Consortium on School Research (Bryk et al., 2010). In Chapter 1 you examined this framework as you were guided to identify all of the tasks, people, or tools in your school that influence these functions (see Figure 1.2). By paying attention to the interactions occurring in your school with regard to these five categories, you were able to recognize the range of undetected or stealth leadership activity in your context that influences these functions.

Now it's worth revisiting those functions and your conjectures about who is currently performing them, in order to identify potential improvements in their co-performance and in what ways additional formal and informal influence could be promoted strategically to enhance those important functions. The Co-Performance Mapping exercise is designed to help you do just that (see Figure 3.2). Sample responses are included in the figure. A blank copy is provided in Appendix A, as well as online.

Figure 3.2 revisits and extends the analysis initiated in Figure 1.2 in service of developing leadership co-performance routines that can help leaders align their efforts and get in sync. In this version, you will reorganize examples of leadership tasks, activities, and tools by the key teacher/leaders involved. In doing so, you will likely recall additional tasks, activities, and routines that can be added to the map. Importantly, you will be able to note who is currently co-performing leadership in the same function areas as others and would benefit from alignment with each other.

FIGURE 3.2 CO-PERFORMANCE MAPPING

In the first column of the table below, list the key teacher/leader roles and teams that you have in your school (e.g., principal, instructional leadership team members, grade-level team members, literacy coach). (You may have identified them in Figure 1.2.) Note that every teacher is likely a member of some team and, as such, could be considered a teacher/leader.

For each teacher/leader role or team, use the remaining columns to list the tasks, activities, or routines with which they are involved related to each leadership function. Include indirect, informal, and unintentional influence on the quality of teaching and learning.

Teacher/ Leaders	Leadership Functions Necessary for Learning					
	School Learning Climate	Professional Capacity	Shared Instructional Expectations	Family and Community Involvement	Student Outcomes	Other
Principal	Sets and reinforces climate expectations	Secures resources for PD Requires PD reports on external PD	Sets and communicates expectations	Communicates school priorities and solicits family and community as partners in addressing them	Leads faculty discussion about annual data results	Locates budget allotment for new instructional materials
Instructional Leadership Team Members		Sets priorities for PD Evaluates PD; sometimes provides it	Coordinates walkthroughs and peer observations		Coordinates school-wide student work portfolio routine	
Grade-Level Team Leaders			Leads LASW	Organizes classroom exhibitions	Facilitates analysis of formative assessments and instructional responses to data	

(continued)

FIGURE 3.2 CO-PERFORMANCE MAPPING continued

Teacher/ Leaders	Leadership Functions Necessary for Learning					Other
	School Learning Climate	Professional Capacity	Shared Instructional Expectations	Family and Community Involvement	Student Outcomes	
Content Leaders/ Department Chairs		Provides content-based coaching to teachers	Lead development of common assessments and curriculum mapping	Math Department Leader: takes lead in organizing Math Night. ELA Department Leader: takes lead in organizing Literacy Night	Monitors academic progress within content area and respond with training or resources	
Parent Council	Leads core values and mission discussion each year	Pays for book club books for teachers		Engages the community	Communicates importance of family conferences	
Faculty (individuals)	Student Council advisor: directs School Site Council in planning assemblies. Ms. Green: regularly offers shout-outs	Book club leaders and participants. Mr. Brown: leaves professional journals in the teachers' room. Mentor teachers that focus on teaching and learning	Bring work to LASW and/or contribute to conversation. Ms. Black: shared her lesson-planning template	Initiating family conferences. Ms. Blanco: attends parent breakfast to support communication with the principal, who doesn't speak Spanish	Determine content of their own Bulletin Boards. Ms. Burgundy: reminds us to disaggregate data and look at subgroup performance	Mr. Grey: retired teacher returns as a volunteer to support curriculum development

1. Review each function (column) in your grid:

- Is each function addressed adequately? Are there gaps and redundancies?
- Are there tasks, activities, tools, systems, and routines in each column that provide opportunities for interaction throughout the year? Or only sporadically?
- Do these interactions have a strong or weak influence on the leadership function?

2. Observe the distribution of teacher/leaders' influence across the grid:

- How aware do you feel teacher/leaders are of the influence they exert within each function?
- To what extent are they aware of who else is influencing this function (intentionally or unintentionally)?
- Are routines in place to ensure communication and coordination among these leaders?
- What actions might be taken to influence the formal distribution of leadership around this leadership function? By whom?
- What actions might be taken to influence the informal distribution of leadership around this leadership function? By whom?

Source: Functions are adapted from *Organizing Schools for Improvement* (Bryk et al., 2010) and the National Center for School Leadership's model of learning-centered leadership (Southworth, 2005).
Note: You can also choose another framework or just identify a leadership function on your own. Be sure to pick one that identifies what has to be accomplished by leadership, not a list of tasks to be done. Another list of leadership functions is found in Copland & Knapp's (2006) *Pathways to Student, Professional and System Learning.* This is a much broader list of functions that includes many with an indirect influence on learning.

Completing this kind of thinking exercise together can help a leadership team to recognize patterns of leadership influence that result in gaps and redundancies and to be more aware of ways these patterns might occur at other levels of leadership (e.g., within a department or grade-level team). Although a team would not use this type of exercise on a routine basis, it could be useful as a planning tool or retreat.

For example, the Pearl Middle School, which is committed to personalized learning, must have some way of preparing the school learning climate, expanding professional capacity for this new work, establishing and communicating about shared instructional expectations, tapping families and community as partners, and monitoring the student outcomes of the new initiative. The Co-Performance Mapping exercise could have helped them to design teams and roles that comprehensively address the various functions required for success, as well as to identify who needs to be talking to whom, and to establish communication routines important for keeping efforts in sync.

Expertise Analysis

When planning starts with the functions—or what we want to accomplish—instead of the people, as traditionally occurs, we can design the work for success. We can think up front about the knowledge, skills, and dispositions that would be required for the work to succeed, and then use that information to make decisions about whether formal or informal roles are needed and how they are organized.

The Expertise We Need

Let's say that a faculty has identified a new priority area: reforming our science curriculum. Before we think about whether an individual is needed to help guide the staff, a committee should be appointed to shepherd this work, or teachers will informally support each other. We should make our best predictions about the work required. What are the tasks, activities, and routines needed? (An organizer like Figure 3.2 may help us to do that.) Then, with these tasks in mind, we're able to think about what expertise would be important to have on hand to accomplish the work skillfully.

The Teacher Leadership Expertise Inventory in Figure 3.3 is a tool that can be used for this type of backward-mapping from the specific school priority area, to the tasks of the leadership functions, to the expertise needed. It contains a list of the wide range of knowledge, skills, and dispositions that teacher leaders might be required to know, do, and espouse across many roles. (For more on teacher leadership skills frameworks, see Figure 3.6.) To address a given school priority area well, which few knowledge, skills, and dispositions are most essential?

FIGURE 3.3 TEACHER LEADERSHIP EXPERTISE INVENTORY

School Priority Area:
Tasks, Activities, and Tools Required:

Keeping the tasks and activities listed above in mind, indicate which of the following are most important to the success of the work.

Knowledge

Knowledge of Students	Professional Knowledge
Knowledge of child development	Knowledge of subject matter content and grade-level standards
Knowledge of children as individuals	Knowledge of content-related and general pedagogical theory
Knowledge of children: special populations and diverse needs	Knowledge of instructional strategies and instructional design
Knowledge of adults	Knowledge of assessment practices and data literacy
Knowledge of adult learning and development	Knowledge of curriculum development and implementation
Knowledge of group and organizational learning	Knowledge of cultural and structural requirements of a productive (safe, collaborative, and engaging) learning environment
Knowledge of families and strategies for engagement/partnership	Knowledge of schools as organizations
Knowledge of the local community and strategies for partnership	Knowledge of school law and education policy

Skills

Building Community and Shared Ownership	Systems Thinking
• Engaging stakeholders, building teams, and forging collaborations • Creating, advocating, and maintaining a shared vision • Building and sustaining trust • Creating and maintaining norms that ensure safety, equity of voice, and culturally responsive interaction	• Communicating within and across teams • Ensuring vertical and horizontal alignment (coherence) of efforts • Accessing, analyzing, and utilizing education research • Interpreting, analyzing, and advocating policy that supports teaching and learning
Managing Groups • Managing and monitoring group dynamics and tone • Maintaining energy and focus • Organizing productive group/work structures • Dealing with resistance or difficult colleagues	**Communication and Advocacy** • Communicating with technology • Communicating with data • Communicating with different audiences • Communicating with clarity, tact, and transparency

(continued)

FIGURE 3.3 TEACHER LEADERSHIP EXPERTISE INVENTORY continued

Skills (continued)

Facilitating Dialogue • Establishing a purpose and process for dialogue • Facilitating reflective dialogue and ensuring continuous group learning • Working through disagreement; managing conflict • Building consensus and facilitating decision making	**Guiding Evidence-Based Decision Making** • Preparing a team for data use • Collecting and interpreting quantitative and qualitative data • Analyzing data with attention to cultural proficiency • Monitoring progress and maintaining focus on continuous improvement
Leading Professional Learning • Applying principles of adult learning • Designing effective professional learning experiences • Leading coaching conversations • Giving feedback	**Self-Care and Growth** • Knowing your own style, strengths, and challenges • Managing the work with balance and efficiency • Depersonalizing anger and negativity • Reflecting; seeking and receiving feedback

Dispositions

Has a growth mindset	Is collaborative
Enjoys working with adults	Is reliable
Accepts and acts on constructive feedback	Is a lifelong learner
Possesses courage to take risks	Is reflective
Does not avoid honest, courageous communication	Is committed to supporting growth of others
Honors all perspectives	Is attuned to relationships
Assumes best intentions	Is interested in larger/bigger picture
Embraces the opportunity to work with those with diverse views	Enjoys challenges
Fosters community	Has passion for topic
Admits when wrong/doesn't know	Values professional expertise

Source: Knowledge and skills are adapted from the Boston Teacher Leadership Certificate Program Skills Framework (Berg, Miller, & Souvanna, 2011). Dispositions are adapted from *Teacher Leader Skills Framework* (Center for Strengthening the Teaching Profession, 2009).

By using the Teacher Leadership Expertise Inventory, teacher/leaders have an overview of the expertise required to move a priority forward. They can identify which teacher/leaders within the professional community have these areas of expertise, and where there are gaps they can proactively seek resources to build capacity in these areas.

If we had a better sense of who is good at what within the faculty, we could think strategically about ways to maximize the leadership influence of teachers. This is counter cultural in many settings. Teachers are expected to be good at everything.

But, in truth, teachers are human, with strengths, challenges, passions, and joys. We have many talents and intelligences, just like students. When we think about students, it's useful to think about *how* they're smart, not *whether* they're smart. What if we took a similar differentiated view of faculty expertise?

The Expertise We Have

The Assets Inventory in Figure 3.4 is a tool that many teacher/leaders have found useful for helping them to consider how the differentiated talents and interests of individuals might be viewed as organizational assets. In Part A, list the names of teacher/leaders (including all administrators) in the first row and identify as column headings the areas of expertise (knowledge and skills, networks, and credentials) that are most important for the school's priorities. These areas of expertise can be drawn from Figure 3.3 as needed. Then track what you know (or can learn through surveys) about expertise on your faculty. For each teacher/leader, insert a "2" if the skill is a marked strength, a "1" if this is a demonstrated skill, or a "0" if you don't know. Once you have completed this part of the inventory, you might stop to look for patterns.

Now, turning to Part B, the "Formal Roles" section, repeat the same list of teacher/leaders in the first column and add your school's teams along the top (as column headings). This time, moving column by column, team by team, insert a "2" to indicate the leader (facilitator) of the team, a "1" to indicate each member of the team, and a "0" for any inactive or nonparticipating members of the team. Again, step back and look for patterns: Who holds many (maybe *too many*) roles? To what extent does each team have the expertise needed to fulfill its primary function? What types of expertise are currently lacking on each team and who, given the information in Part A, might be a good candidate to provide it?

The Assets Inventory in Figure 3.4 can be populated with data in various ways. Principals might attempt to complete it based on their own knowledge and observations (though they often find they are unable to do so). Leadership team members might complete it together, or they might do so individually and then compare their results. Many schools I work with have faculty members self-report their areas of strength via an online survey. Instead of using the 2-1-0 rating scale, schools sometimes simply ask teachers to identify two or three areas of strength. The level of relational trust must be considered here. Will teachers trust that this is an opportunity to improve collaboration and not a "gotcha" move, with the results showing up on their evaluation or with their subsequently being "volunteered" for lots of extra duties? To truly trust, they will want to know what will be done with the data. The questions at the bottom of Figure 3.4 offer a window into the strategic planning that's possible with these data.

FIGURE 3.4 ASSETS INVENTORY, PART A: EXPERTISE

List all members of the team or faculty in the first column.

Use the codes provided to indicate the strengths of each member. This can be based on member self-reports, peer reports of each other's strengths, or leadership team estimations. Then indicate any network affiliations or credentials members have that may indicate additional relevant expertise, experience, or opportunities to learn.

| Names | Knowledge and Skills — Codes: 2 = strength; 1 = demonstrated; 0 = don't know/no evidence | | | | | | | | | | | | Networks and Credentials | |
	Knowledge of student development and special populations	ELA knowledge	Math knowledge	Instructional repertoire	Skill in managing and monitoring student learning	Skill in reflective practice	Collaboration skills	Team facilitation skills	Communication skills	Skills for facilitating adult learning	Facility with data	Social/political capital	Membership in Professional Associations or Networks	Special Skills, Certifications, and/or Training
Araujo	2	1	1	2	1	1	1	2	1	2	0	2		
Brown	1	1	2	1	1	0	1	1	0	1	2	0		
Charles	1	2	1	1	0	1	2	0	0	0	0	1	NCTE	
DeLeon	2	1	1	2	2	1	2	1	1	1	2	2		NBCT
Evergreen	1	1	0	0	1	1	1	1	2	1	0	2	TLI	
Fiore	0	0	1	1	1	0	1	2	1	2	0	1		SRI Facilitator
Gianopolous	0	0	2	0	0	0	1	0	0	0	2	0		
Harvey	0	0	0	0	0	0	0	0	0	0	0	0	ASCD	admin cert
Ianello	1	1	2	1	1	1	1	1	1	1	2	1		
Jacques	2	2	1	2	1	2	0	0	0	0	0	0		CAGS: literacy
Kallamata	0	0	0	0	0	0	0	1	1	0	0	2		
Longo	1	1	1	2	1	0	1	1	0	2	0	1	ASCD	Fluent in Spanish
Ming	1	0	0	0	0	0	2	2	2	1	0	2		

Review the sample data provided above:
- What do you notice? What patterns do you see?
- To what extent do strengths align with student needs and school priorities in your context?
- How might teachers' strengths be utilized as assets throughout this school?
- How might teachers' expertise be cultivated strategically to meet local needs and priorities?

FIGURE 3.4 ASSETS INVENTORY, PART B: FORMAL ROLES

After examining the data in Part A, copy the names in the first column of Part B. In addition, list all of the school's key teams in the Team Assignments row.

Then use the space and codes provided to indicate members' individual formal roles and team assignments.

Names	Formal Roles (e.g., literacy coach, lead teacher, department head, teacher-in-charge, mentor)	Instructional Leadership Team	School Site Council/Governing Board	ELL Language Acquisition Team	School Support Team	School Climate Team	Data Team	9th Grade Team	10th Grade Team	11th Grade Team	12th Grade Team	ELA Team	Math Team
Araujo	ELL Liaison, Mentor	1		2	1		1	1					
Brown		1						2					1
Charles		1						1				1	
DeLeon	Lead Teacher, Mentor	2			1	1	1		1			1	
Evergreen		1			2				1				
Fiore						2	1		1				
Gianopolous			1						1				1
Harvey										1			
Ianello										1			1
Jacques	Mentor				1					1		1	
Kallamata			1							2			
Longo											1		
Ming		1	1		1		2				2		

Looking across Parts A and B, review the sample data provided above:

- Who would you ask to be the team leader for grade 10?
- Your ELA coach is available to work with only one grade-level team. Which one?
- You and the ELL department liaison are looking to form a new ELL Language Acquisition Team. Who do you tap?

Consider this tool:

- What might be involved in completing this inventory in your school? Who should be involved?
- How might you adapt this tool for your school?
- How could this tool support your school to better activate—and cultivate—teachers' expertise as an asset toward greater student success?

Although this exercise could be used to recruit teachers for specific roles and teams, it is even more useful for recognizing the different expertise that every teacher has and for allowing teacher/leaders to think differently together about teachers' current roles and teams. It allows them to consider the range of expertise available among the faculty, to envision a strategic redesign of how that expertise is deployed as a resource for school priorities (discussed in Chapter 4), and to consider capacity-building investments. A blank copy of Figure 3.4 is provided in Appendix A, as well as online.

Building Capacity for Leadership

Teachers exercise leadership every day as leaders of their classrooms. However, leading a meeting of adults who don't want to be there, supporting colleagues to analyze and understand data they may be afraid to look at, or getting teammates to collaborate on a task they have been avoiding presents unique challenges that require new skills. Informal leadership takes skill, too. Speaking up when a colleague blames students and families for student learning gaps, resisting a team member's toxic attitude, and generating excitement about an upcoming challenge are all moves that could exert a positive influence on teaching and learning if teachers know how to make them. Although most administrators have been exposed to a knowledge base on how to do these things effectively, it has largely been left out of teacher education. In general, leadership standards for teachers and leadership standards for administrators have developed in separate silos.

If teacher/leaders are going to work together and succeed together, it makes sense that they should spend some time learning together so that they can share at least some of the same mental models, touchstone texts, and language. Existing leadership frameworks can help us identify the leadership learning needs that teachers and administrators have in common. From there we can envision new possibilities for how they can strengthen their expertise in these areas together.

Leadership Frameworks

In 2015, a cross-stakeholder group of educational leaders convened to revisit and update the voluntary school leadership standards developed in 1996 and updated in 2008 by the Interstate School Leaders Licensure Consortium (ISLLC). This recent effort, led by the Council of Chief State School Officers together with eight organizations that make up the National Policy Board for Educational Administration, was informed by a decade of new research on school leadership and engaged the input of over 1,000 practicing principals and superintendents.

Although ISLLC standards have generally been used to guide the development of school administrators, this latest iteration—which was created with a new focus on putting students at the center and ensuring they are prepared for the 21st century—describes 10 areas of educational leadership to which teachers stand to make important contributions.

Figure 3.5 lists the 10 standards with their descriptors. Given teachers' unique positions in schools—at the nexus of where teaching and learning happen and alongside their peers—what unique contribution might teachers make to each standard?

FIGURE 3.5 PROFESSIONAL STANDARDS FOR EDUCATIONAL LEADERS

Standard 1. Mission, Vision, and Core Values	Effective educational leaders develop, advocate, and enact a shared mission, vision, and core values of high-quality education and academic success and well-being of each student.
Standard 2. Ethics and Professional Norms	Effective educational leaders act ethically and according to professional norms to promote each student's academic success and well-being.
Standard 3. Equity and Cultural Responsiveness	Effective educational leaders strive for equity of educational opportunity and culturally responsive practices to promote each student's academic success and well-being.
Standard 4. Curriculum, Instruction, and Assessment	Effective educational leaders develop and support intellectually rigorous and coherent systems of curriculum, instruction, and assessment to promote each student's academic success and well-being.
Standard 5. Community of Care and Support for Students	Effective educational leaders cultivate an inclusive, caring, and supportive school community that promotes the academic success and well-being of each student.
Standard 6. Professional Capacity of School Personnel	Effective educational leaders develop the professional capacity and practice of school personnel to promote each student's academic success and well-being.
Standard 7. Professional Community for Teachers and Staff	Effective educational leaders foster a professional community of teachers and other professional staff to promote each student's academic success and well-being.
Standard 8. Meaningful Engagement of Families and Community	Effective educational leaders engage families and the community in meaningful, reciprocal, and mutually beneficial ways to promote each student's academic success and well-being.
Standard 9. Operations and Management	Effective educational leaders manage school operations and resources to promote each student's academic success and well-being.
Standard 10. School Improvement	Effective educational leaders act as agents of continuous improvement to promote each student's academic success and well-being.

Source: National Policy Board for Educational Administration (2015).

Note: The full document also lists for each standard some of the salient elements of work involved and is available from http://npbea.org/.

From a distributed perspective, teachers routinely influence every one of these standards—in intentional and unintentional ways, in positive and negative ways. It makes sense that an investment in teachers' leadership knowledge and skills would make it all the more likely that they will exert an intentional, positive influence in these areas. In recent years, teachers have had increasing opportunities to do so through teacher leadership programs.

Whether structured as part of a fellowship program, a master's degree, district-based PD, or an online micro-credential; whether focused on improving instruction, changing policy, transforming culture, or fueling organizational improvement in their schools; and whether teachers are selected through application or are assigned, recruited, or invited to participate, opportunities for teachers to strengthen their leadership skills take many forms (Berg & Zhao, 2017). Such programs recognize (1) that many teachers want to make a difference beyond their own classrooms and (2) that ensuring they have the skills needed to do that well benefits everyone.

In the past decade, several attempts have been made to define the knowledge base needed for teacher leadership. The undertaking is complicated. The tasks of teacher leadership roles vary widely, and the knowledge and skills needed for success are often role-specific. The expertise required to successfully lead a whole-faculty meeting to analyze schoolwide trends in student achievement data is different from the expertise needed to be a mentor. Similarly, the expertise required to be an effective mentor varies depending on whether one is an induction coach working with cohorts of new teachers or a consulting teacher working one-on-one with a struggling veteran in a peer assistance and review (PAR) program.

Nevertheless, three frameworks for what teacher leaders should know and do are used widely (see Figure 3.6).

In 2009, the Center for Strengthening the Teaching Profession (CSTP) convened teacher leaders from Washington state to identify key teacher leader roles and describe the knowledge, skills, and dispositions needed across those roles. They published the *Teacher Leadership Skills Framework,* which organizes the knowledge and skills teacher leaders need into five main categories. As the first comprehensive effort of this kind, CSTP's Teacher Leadership Skills Framework has been adopted, adapted, and used as a model for many subsequent efforts.

In 2011, a Teacher Leadership Exploratory Consortium, convened by Educational Testing Service, published the *Teacher Leader Model Standards.* Created by a multistakeholder group of teachers, school administrators, and others representing unions, policy organizations, and institutions of higher education, this document identifies seven domains in which teachers might lead and the types of actions that might be important for each. This model was published just in time to inform a

FIGURE 3.6 TEACHER LEADERSHIP FRAMEWORKS

There have been several attempts to list and categorize the knowledge, skills, and dispositions that teacher leaders must master to be accomplished teacher leaders. Here are some widely used frameworks that are publicly accessible.

Teacher Leadership Skills Framework
Center for Strengthening the Teaching Profession (2009)

1. Working with adult learners
2. Communication
3. Collaborative work
4. Knowledge of content and pedagogy
5. Systems thinking

Teacher Leader Model Standards
Teacher Leadership Exploratory Consortium (2011)

1. Fostering a collaborative culture to support educator development and student learning
2. Accessing and using research to improve practice and student learning
3. Promoting professional learning for continuous improvement
4. Facilitating improvements in instruction and student learning
5. Promoting the use of assessments and data for school and district improvement
6. Improving outreach and collaboration with families and community
7. Advocating for student learning and the profession

Teacher Leadership Initiative Competencies*
Center for Teacher Quality, National Board for Professional Teaching Standards, and National Education Association (2014)

Overarching Competencies
1a. Reflective practice
1b. Personal effectiveness
1c. Interpersonal effectiveness
1d. Communication
1e. Continuing learning and education
1f. Group processes
1g. Adult learning
1h. Technological facility
1i. Organizing and advocacy

Pathway Competencies
Instructional Leadership
2a. Coaching/mentoring
2b. Collaborative relationships
2c. Community

Policy Leadership
3a. Implementation
3b. Advocacy
3c. Policy making
3d. Engagement

Association Leadership
4a. Leading with vision
4b. Leading with skill
4c. Organizing/advocacy
4d. Building capacity
4e. Community/culture

*Due to be revised in 2018. Visit www.nea.org for updates.

---

major national expansion of graduate programs for teacher leaders, as well as new state-level endorsements.

In 2014, the Center for Teaching Quality, National Board for Professional Teaching Standards, and National Education Association (NEA) collaborated to extend the Teacher Leader Model Standards work. They invited teams of teacher leaders to devise a set of *Teacher Leader Competencies* intended to guide teachers' reflection and development as leaders. The resulting document organizes the competencies into four groups: overarching competencies, as well as competencies specific to three main pathways. Two factors propelled these standards into widespread use. First, the NEA supports hundreds of teachers each year to partic-ipate as fellows in the Teacher Leadership Institute, through which they are sup-ported to study the standards, develop their skills, and demonstrate them through a portfolio and capstone project. Second, these competencies are accompanied by a tool that describes what each competency might look like at four stages of devel-opment: emerging, developing, performing, and transforming. Many districts and programs have found this tool to be useful in a practical way.

Looking across these three skills frameworks (see Figure 3.6), we see patterns in their areas of emphasis. Teacher leaders need to know how to build community and shared ownership, as well as manage groups to be productive in working toward a shared vision. They might be called on to facilitate the kind of dialogue that can support reflection and effective decision making, or to lead powerful professional learning. They must understand their teams and schools as part of a system and communicate clearly and effectively with all throughout that system. When deci-sions must be made, teacher leaders guide others in using evidence to inform those decisions. Finally, teacher leaders must take care of themselves and their own need to thrive as learners. The importance of these skill areas is corroborated across these well-referenced frameworks, but these documents each stop short of describing what teacher leaders need to *learn*. To build competency in the identified domains and competencies, an inventory of teachable skills is needed. We know that teacher leaders need to be able to collaborate and foster a collaborative culture among oth-ers, but what do they need to *learn* in order to do these things?

The Teacher Leadership Expertise Inventory (see Figure 3.3) includes such a list. It identifies the wide range of knowledge, skills, and dispositions that teachers would have to learn to be competent in the domains of the various teacher leader frameworks. The Expertise Inventory encompasses the knowledge base on teach-ing, as well as role-relevant components of the knowledge base on leadership.

In fact, these same knowledge, skills, and dispositions are important when addressing the Professional Standards for Educational Leaders (see Figure 3.5). Figure 3.7 illustrates this point by demonstrating alignment of the "skills" portion of the Teacher Leader Expertise Inventory with these professional standards.

Learning Together

Teachers/leaders often learn the lion's share of their leadership knowledge and skills simply by jumping in and leading. Trial by fire is an effective but sometimes cruel teacher. Fortunately, most teacher/leaders are resourceful learners who, when faced with a challenge, will find the resources to learn how to attack it. They'll ask someone; find a book, website, or webinar; or maybe even find a graduate course

FIGURE 3.7 TEACHER LEADERSHIP SKILLS ALIGNMENT WITH THE PROFESSIONAL STANDARDS FOR EDUCATIONAL LEADERS

The table identifies skills from the Teacher Leader Expertise Inventory (Figure 3.3) that align with the Professional Standards for Educational Leaders (Figure 3.5). There are known strategies that can be learned and practiced for each of these skills. What might be the impact on the effectiveness and efficiency of our school leadership systems if more teachers (and administrators) were supported to learn and practice these skills? And to do so together?

Professional Standards for Educational Leaders		Skills from the Teacher Leader Expertise Inventory
Standard 1. Mission, Vision, and Core Values	Effective educational leaders develop, advocate, and enact a shared mission, vision, and core values of high-quality educa-tion and academic success and well-being of each student.	• Creating, advocating, and maintaining a shared vision
Standard 2. Ethics and Professional Norms	Effective educational leaders act ethically and according to pro-fessional norms to promote each student's academic success and well-being.	• Building and sustaining trust • Knowing your own style, strengths, and challenges • Managing the work with balance and efficiency • Depersonalizing anger and negativity • Seeking and receiving feedback • Communicating with clarity, tact, and transparency
Standard 3. Equity and Cultural Responsiveness	Effective educational leaders strive for equity of educational opportu-nity and culturally responsive prac-tices to promote each student's academic success and well-being.	• Creating and maintaining norms that ensure safety, equity of voice, and culturally responsive interaction • Analyzing data with attention to cultural proficiency
Standard 4. Curricu-lum, Instruction, and Assessment	Effective educational leaders develop and support intellectually rigorous and coherent systems of curriculum, instruction, and assessment to promote each student's academic success and well-being.	• Ensuring vertical and horizontal alignment (coherence) of efforts • Accessing, analyzing, and utilizing education research • Preparing a team for data use • Collecting and interpreting quantitative and quali-tative data
Standard 5. Community of Care and Support for Students	Effective educational leaders cultivate an inclusive, caring, and supportive school community that promotes the academic success and well-being of each student.	• Monitoring progress and maintaining focus on continuous improvement
Standard 6. Professional Capacity of School Personnel	Effective educational leaders develop the professional capacity and practice of school personnel to promote each student's academic success and well-being.	• Applying principles of adult learning • Designing effective professional learning experiences • Leading coaching conversations • Giving feedback • Dealing with resistance or difficult colleagues

(continued)

FIGURE 3.7 TEACHER LEADERSHIP SKILLS ALIGNMENT WITH THE
PROFESSIONAL STANDARDS FOR EDUCATIONAL LEADERS continued

Professional Standards for Educational Leaders		Skills from the Teacher Leader Expertise Inventory
Standard 7. Professional Community for Teachers and Staff	Effective educational leaders foster a professional community of teachers and other professional staff to promote each student's academic success and well-being.	• Managing and monitoring group dynamics and tone • Maintaining energy and focus • Establishing a purpose and process for dialogue • Facilitating reflective dialogue and ensuring continuous group learning • Working through disagreement; managing conflict • Building consensus and facilitating decision making
Standard 8. Meaningful Engagement of Families and Community	Effective educational leaders engage families and the community in meaningful, reciprocal, and mutually beneficial ways to promote each student's academic success and well-being.	• Engaging stakeholders, building teams, and forging collaborations • Communicating with different audiences
Standard 9. Operations and Management	Effective educational leaders manage school operations and resources to promote each student's academic success and well-being.	• Organizing productive group/work structures • Communicating with technology • Communicating with data
Standard 10. School Improvement	Effective educational leaders act as agents of continuous improvement to promote each student's academic success and well-being.	• Communicating within and across teams • Interpreting, analyzing, and advocating policy that supports teaching and learning

that can teach them what they need to know to succeed. As we think about strategically maximizing the leadership capacity of all educators—teachers and school administrators alike—thinking strategically about leadership skill development is important, too. Leadership development is too important to leave it to chance or to the hope that educators will pursue it in their spare time. The ideas and tools presented in this chapter can help teacher/leaders envision practical new leadership learning opportunities they can pursue together.

One opportunity is for teacher/leaders to use the Teacher Leader Expertise Inventory (see Figure 3.3) to identify one or two specific skills relevant to the work they are already doing together, and to be intentional about their actions and reflections in these areas. John Dewey is often cited as reminding us that "we do not learn from experience; we learn from reflecting on experience." Sharing common language for the leadership skills that make up our leadership practice helps us to name, isolate, and think together about our practice of those skills. The Expertise Inventory can serve as a menu of sorts for choosing skills worth attention. Teacher/

leaders can build time to reflect together about their targeted skill into a regular check-in meeting, an online exchange, or even the end of a team meeting agenda.

Another opportunity presents itself with the Assets Inventory (see Figure 3.4). Teacher/leaders have much they can learn from each other's strengths. But how would they know what their colleagues are good at that might be useful to them? The Assets Inventory can be populated with selected skills from the Teacher Leader Expertise Inventory. Once teacher/leaders use it to self-report their areas of strength and the areas in which they want to grow, it would be possible to create complementary pairs in which each member has something to learn from the other. They can share strategies, observe one another, and reflect together.

Finally, teacher/leaders can engage in formal learning opportunities together. From conferences to course work to webinars, professional learning opportunities that are pursued together offer greater potential for lasting impact. The social interaction in and around the learning experience will help reinforce ideas, challenge thinking, and make the experience memorable. Joint participation will help teacher/leaders to feel accountable for applying their learning and enable them to provide site-based support to one another when needed. As previously mentioned, leadership development for teachers has been conceptualized using different frameworks than leadership development for leaders. Figure 3.7 provides a window into the value of bringing the two together and may suggest opportunities to do so.

When multiple teacher/leaders are co-performing leadership skillfully, there is great potential for a school's collective leadership capacity to have a positive impact on shared goals. Teacher/leaders must consider how their combined actions will address important leadership functions and school priorities, who should be doing what, and how they will learn to do it well. This is necessary but not sufficient for success. They also need to be prepared to manage the socioemotional and logistical changes that naturally occur with this shift in strategy. They need to create a culture that can support teacher leadership, the subject of the next chapter.

A RETURN TO PEARL MIDDLE SCHOOL

Upon their return to school, teacher/leaders at Pearl Middle School quickly recognized that they were not in sync. The staff dedicated a half-day to coordinating their efforts for the move toward personalized learning. They revisited the data and shared values that had pointed them toward personalized learning in the first place (see Chapter 2). Then, in groups, they read some grounding articles recommended by the tech liaison and a chapter from the principal's purchased book, to refine their shared vision about what personalized learning would look like if it was successful in their school. Next, they created a co-performance map (see Figure 3.2) by writing the key activities they had initiated thus far on sticky notes and collecting them on chart paper labeled "Leadership Functions." Under the heading "Professional Capacity," the literacy coach posted that she had agendas planned for after-school professional development, and when she saw that the dates of the graduate course the 8th grade team had started would conflict with her plans, she indicated "Dates: To Be Determined." The principal's book and the tech liaison's articles were listed here, too. The 8th grade team members posted the strategies they learned for managing personalized learning under the heading "Shared Instructional Expectations," and they took note of the tech liaison's sticky note about a Google Classroom under the same heading. "This could be an opportunity for collaboration," they both thought. Instructional resources such as apps and Chromebooks were listed here, too. Standing back and noting gaps, teacher/leaders then brainstormed and posted ideas for how the other leadership functions might be addressed. The resulting chart would facilitate conversation and coordination among the key functions needed for success.

There was much to be done, and they decided it would be addressed most efficiently through teams. They created a professional development team charged with deepening understanding about personalized learning throughout the faculty, and a tech support team to ensure faculty felt supported to be successful with the wide array of new online tools. They used the Teacher Leadership Expertise Inventory (see Figure 3.3) together with the Assets Inventory (see Figure 3.4) to staff those teams with the expertise needed for them to succeed. Then, recognizing the importance of staying in sync and growing their own skills for leading this work, the two teams came together monthly to revisit their co-performance map (see Figure 3.2), to reflect on their progress and next steps, and to practice together one or two key leadership skills (see Figure 3.7) that could help them take this work to the next level.

Reflection

1. Review your responses to the context questions at the beginning of this chapter. What new reflections do you have, and what possibilities for action do you see?
2. How might the ideas and strategies from this chapter help teacher/leaders in your school to co-perform leadership more skillfully?

Culture of Teacher Leadership

IN YOUR CONTEXT . . .

- What aspects of your school's culture and structure lead teachers to unintentionally influence the quality of teaching and learning beyond their own classrooms?
- How clear and shared are educators' understandings of teacher/leader roles and what teams do?
- How do teacher/leaders and teams document and share their work so that others can stay in sync and build on it?

Taking a strategic approach to teacher leadership can be a big change for some schools. The notion that teachers' influence beyond their own classrooms might be encouraged and even supported can be a cause for pause or even stress for both teachers and administrators. It can run counter to cultural norms that have developed about how much input teachers will accept into their professional decision making and from whom, it can conflict with preexisting structures that shape whether teachers have the time and space to interact and to influence each other, and it can cause confusion in professional identity: Will teachers' effectiveness in the classroom drive them out of it? What should be a teacher leader's role? What are the boundaries of authority? Who decides?

This chapter addresses the key issues teachers face regarding role clarity within a context of teacher leadership. It also provides tools that principals and other leaders can use to manage this change.

WESTLUND K-8 SCHOOL

Westlund K–8 School is a large neighborhood school that serves as a hub of activity for the community. Families know they can come weekly to access the mobile food pantry, monthly to drop in on a visiting dental clinician, frequently for parenting workshops, and any time after school to use the community pool. These wraparound resources draw families to the school and support them to feel comfortable there. The teacher-led Climate and Culture Team made this observation and wanted to build on it to draw parents in more deeply as partners in their children's education. They invited the school's newly hired part-time family engagement coordinator to join their next meeting.

The team, consisting of three 4th grade teachers, two 2nd grade teachers, the middle school learning specialist, and the assistant principal, took up this topic at a September meeting. Unfortunately, the family engagement coordinator couldn't make it. The team moved ahead with brainstorming meaningful ways for teachers and families to partner. These included giving families strategies they could use to support their own children with homework and suggestions of things to do on weekends to explore curriculum-related extensions as a family. They also included ideas for drawing family members as resources into classroom experiences, for example, to send in videos of themselves telling favorite family stories, to come share history and artifacts from places they have been, or to participate on a panel to discuss how school prepared them for their current careers. When the Climate and Culture Team shared these ideas with the faculty and invited grade-level teams to pick one to pursue, most teams greeted the idea with enthusiasm.

The middle school team combined forces to organize a career panel assembly to which they would invite parents to speak. They wanted to build on a similar classroom-based event organized by last year's 7th grade teacher, but she had left the school and there was no record of what she had done, so they had to start from scratch. The 4th grade team created an elaborate plan to replace Math Night with a Round-the-World Night to complement their global studies unit, though when they shared their idea with the principal, she determined that Math Night was required and non-negotiable. Could they hold the new event during the day? The 2nd grade team organized a classroom breakfast to provide each family with a customized list of reading strategies they could use to help their child move to the next reading level. They asked the family engagement coordinator to make calls to invite families, but she had not understood phone-calling to be her role and didn't appreciate being assigned this task by teachers. In fact, she had spent her first weeks talking with the district's College and Career Readiness Office about planning a schoolwide Career Day. Perhaps that was now redundant in light of the new middle school plans. The grades with no teachers on the Climate and Culture Team were not feeling motivated or accountable to do anything. In fact, one grade-level team questioned why a "Climate and Culture Team" was telling them what to do with families.

The issue of authority is a tricky one when it comes to teacher leadership. Is the teacher leader *asking* me to do something or *telling* me to do it? Can the teacher leader do that? Is this a helpful collegial recommendation or an intrusion on my autonomy? And what influences my feelings about it?

Research suggests that teachers' understandings of their roles in schools are largely influenced by their supervisors (Bacharach, Bamberger, & Mitchell, 1990). The clearer administrators can be about role-related information the better, not only for teachers holding formal roles but also for teachers who informally influence their colleagues or are influenced by them. Whether those expectations and roles are defined by the principal or determined collaboratively with teachers, clear communication about roles and expectations reduces stress on everyone. The message principals send about the importance, power, and authority of these roles and expectations is vitally important for everyone during the socioemotional adjustment teachers and other leaders are making to a new way of being together (Hart, 1994).

Teachers' roles are also influenced by their organizational contexts (Smylie & Denny, 1990). If we'd like teachers to influence each other in positive ways, we should think about how the environment can be organized to increase the quantity and quality of their interaction. Teacher/leaders can use the ideas and tools in this chapter to increase the likelihood of influencing each other in intentional, positive ways through both informal and formal roles, including as team members.

Creating a Culture of Teacher Leadership

We know that leadership occurs through interaction. Therefore, a culture of teacher leadership depends on teachers being willing and able to interact with one another. In fact, it should be possible to create an environment in which teachers are regularly interacting in ways that push each other's thinking and move the school forward. In the context of adopting a new curriculum, for example, one could imagine teachers influencing each other in various informal ways, as they ask and answer each other's questions, share resources and reflections on how they worked, and stop in to each other's classrooms to see how it is going. This is a culture of informal teacher leadership, which doesn't require designated roles.

Informal Teacher Leadership

Informal teacher leadership can be facilitated by strategic moves of formal or administrative leaders, such as by organizing schedule and space allocation to encourage interaction. If teachers' schedules don't align and their paths never cross, they are unlikely to influence one another. Similarly, if teachers have ready access to data, professional literature, and school plans, when they do interact, they are more likely to find their conversations informed by these resources. School administrators can make sure teachers have such access. Too often when teachers have a professional dilemma, they don't know who to go to or how to reach those individuals quickly. Further, they may not feel safe enough to ask a question that might expose their vulnerabilities. Helping the faculty know each other's strengths and setting up structures and a culture that make it easy and likely for teachers to feel they can approach each other for help is important for encouraging and enabling informal teacher leadership. Teacher/leaders can consider the following as they reflect on whether the conditions in their school are maximally conducive to a culture of teacher leadership and what role they can play in creating such conditions:

1. Where might regular conversations about teaching and learning occur in my school?
2. What informs the focus of teachers' conversations about teaching and learning in my school?
3. Do teachers in my school feel they have permission from one another to discuss the teaching and learning in each other's classrooms?
4. How do teachers in my school know which colleagues to tap when they have a question about teaching and learning?
5. How do teachers in my school get a question about teaching or learning answered quickly?
6. How do teachers in my school learn about what research and best practice have to say when they have a teaching or learning question?
7. Where and when might teachers in my school engage with family and community members in ways that help fuel and inform conversations about improved teaching and learning?

8. Do teachers in my school feel psychologically safe enough to take the risks required to make real change and improvement?

One might ask whether information leadership can realistically be tapped in service of a school priority. If by "informal" we mean that roles are not formally designated, compensated, or acknowledged, then it's true that no traditional accountability measures would be guiding the quality and quantity of interactions. However, formal teacher/leaders, especially principals, play an important role in whether it is likely—or even possible—that teachers will informally influence teaching and learning beyond their own classrooms. The sample strategies in Figure 4.1 can help. In such contexts, leaders have created a teacher leadership culture.

Teacher Leadership Through Teams

Sometimes teacher/leaders determine that formal teams are needed. In establishing these teams, agreements about the work must be laid out clearly. This is for the benefit of team members, as well as for everyone in the community who may be working with them. The community must be clear on what should (or should not) be expected from team members.

The Team Design Tool in Figure 4.2 supports school principals to collaborate with teams in shaping their own charge. It creates a space for principals, with their positional authority, knowledge of the big picture, and responsibility for any resources required, to clearly lay out what is and is not up for discussion. Is the team required to meet every Tuesday, or is that up to the group? Are we making decisions about new family engagement events, or making recommendations for another committee to consider? Clarifying what is "fixed" and what is "flexible" allows all to recognize the extent of the team's discretion and it can allow the principal to feel more confident about sharing autonomy with teams. It clarifies boundaries and distinguishes what teams are being told from what they are being asked. A blank copy of the Team Design Tool is provided in Appendix A, as well as online.

For a new team, typically the principal presents a draft of this document for discussion with the team, and the team is able to weigh in with questions, concerns, and suggestions for improvement. If the team has already been established, it's an enlightening exercise to have members fill out the Team Design Tool and then compare understandings before agreeing on a final version. Then, since work does not always unfold as planned, the team should commit to revisiting the document halfway through the year and discussing adjustments. Over

FIGURE 4.1 CONDITIONS CONDUCIVE TO A CULTURE OF TEACHER LEADERSHIP

After reflecting on the evaluation questions with your team, prioritize a few conditions for improvement and use the sample strategies provided to create an action plan.

Condition	Questions for Evaluating Condition	Sample Strategies for Creating Condition
A. Strategic Teaming	**Where might regular conversations about teaching and learning occur in my school?** Be sure there is a venue and routine that make it easy for conversations about teaching and learning to occur. Establishing nested systems of teams ensures there is time and space to discuss priorities at all levels (the classroom, team, school level) AND among them.	A1. Align schedules to make it possible for teachers with the same assignment or students to spend time together (e.g., classroom visits, shadowing, curriculum planning, meeting about student needs) A2. Provide collaborative workspace (e.g., team offices or workspace in a teacher's room, so that teachers will plan together, not alone) A3. Have grade-level team representatives form a school-level instructional leadership team and/or a vertical curriculum alignment team A4. Use staff meetings as a collaboration time, instead of as time for disseminating information
B. Data Routines	**What informs the focus of teachers' conversations about teaching and learning in my school?** Be sure you have routines and data systems that enable teachers to regularly review evidence of teaching and learning within and beyond their own classrooms.	B1. Ensure easy access to data training to use district or state data warehouse, hardware and software, filing cabinets, and so on B2. Create a culture of practice with frequent walk-throughs, instructional rounds, peer observations, videotaping, and so on B3. Provide time and training (and the expectation) for teams to engage in data-based inquiry B4. Model evidence-based decision-making and evidence-based discussions B5. Provide time and templates to support peer observation (e.g., guiding questions) B6. Provide time and training for teams to skillfully create common formative assessments (e.g., guiding questions) B7. Encourage teachers to observe and support each other (e.g., provide coverage, video technology)
C. Culture of Shared Ownership	**Do teachers in my school feel they have permission from one another to discuss the teaching and learning in each other's classrooms?** Be sure to create a culture of shared ownership for student learning AND adult learning throughout the school. This requires trust and a shared vision. It requires risk taking and courage.	C1. Communicate and model this expectation regularly C2. Use language of shared ownership (e.g., "our kids") C3. Model and expect members of the community to learn and use names (all students and adults) C4. Establish routines that reinforce shared ownership (inter-classroom visits, portfolios, ways for teachers to learn the names of students they don't have, etc.), including across grades, subjects, special programs, and so on C5. Establish routines that provide teachers with opportunities to show what they are learning, to help each other, and to ask for help C6. Reduce pressures that encourage competition (e.g., merit pay, public comparison of growth scores) C7. Develop and practice norms for having a growth mindset and giving and receiving growth-oriented feedback
D. Inventory of Professional Expertise	**How do teachers in my school know which colleagues to tap when they have a question about teaching and learning?*** Be sure there are ways for teachers to know what everyone else in the building is good at. *This is especially important in a school with high turnover (of teaching and leadership staff)*	D1. Establish meeting routines that enable teachers to share classroom successes and other professional accomplishments so that they see each other's strengths D2. Protect time for those engaged in external PD to come back and share with the staff D3. Survey the staff to identify who is willing to be a go-to person and for what area of instructional expertise D4. Organize learning walks and cross-classroom visits among the faculty D5. Use staff meeting time to allow staff to discuss current topics in education and share professional experiences from beyond school

FIGURE 4.1   CONDITIONS CONDUCIVE TO A CULTURE OF TEACHER LEADERSHIP continued

Condition	Questions for Evaluating Condition	Sample Strategies for Creating Condition
E. Communication Structures	**How do teachers in my school get a question about teaching or learning answered quickly?** Be sure there are tools or systems that enable teachers who have a question about instruction to get it answered quickly by a colleague who might know the answer.	E1. Set up e-mail groups, blogs, or listservs, grouping teachers by expertise E2. Encourage/model a culture of posting and responding to each other's online questions E3. Maintain culture of active mailboxes E4. Establish a 24-hour board (bulletin board that must be checked by all at least once every 24 hours) E5. Establish Q&A section in daily or weekly school memo E6. Clarify when (and how) coaches are available
F. Access to Professional Knowledge Base	**How do teachers in my school learn about what research and best practice have to say when they have a teaching or learning question?** Be sure resources are available for teachers to use to identify answers to questions they cannot address themselves and to get information that will keep them abreast of the latest practice advances.	F1. Establish and maintain a professional library; build routines for sharing what's new, relevant, and being used F2. Obtain school subscriptions to key relevant publications F3. Provide PD on using freely available resources (e.g., accessing education research online with a public library card) F4. Encourage staff to initiate professional book clubs F5. Include research in weekly e-mail/memo that is relevant to current practice F6. Read/respond to articles/research in department or staff meetings
G. Involvement of Family and Community	**Where and when might teachers in my school engage with family and community members in ways that help fuel and inform conversations about improved teaching and learning?** Be sure the school has routines that make it easy for teachers to build relationships with parents around student learning, and to see whether they are aligned with the same aims and values around teaching and learning as family and the community.	G1. Foster parent-teacher collaboration within school-level teams such as School Site Council, grant activities, and so on G2. Establish book groups or forums in which teachers and parents jointly consider education questions such as, "What do we believe is a well-educated child?" G3. Ensure family and community members have regular opportunities to engage with teachers around academic performances (e.g., looking at student work together or family learning walk) G4. Create ways for families to respond to school and classroom newsletters G5. Cultivate monthly family curriculum nights or parent-teacher workshops that place teachers, leaders, and parents in a position to learn from each other
H. Safety	**Do teachers feel psychologically safe enough to take the risks required to make real change and improvement?** The purpose of teacher leadership should be improvement, and improvement doesn't happen without change. But change is scary, and perceived challenges can easily seem to outweigh potential benefits.	H1. Be consistent about establishing, monitoring, and revisiting group norms among the faculty H2. Establish a rapport to facilitate open communication H3. Clarify expectations from suggestions H4. Model risk-taking and make learning-from-error public H5. Model and encourage self-evaluation, including solicitation of feedback H6. Establish check-in routines with teacher/leaders for proactive, two-way dialogue H7. When giving feedback, separate the quality of the experiment from the results; focus on what was learned from the process of the experiment H8. In an after-action review, avoid blaming individuals; consider the system's contributions and be open to organizational adjustments

FIGURE 4.2 TEAM DESIGN TOOL

Use this tool to clarify assumptions and make agreements about the boundaries of a team's authority. Details in the "Fixed" column describe nonnegotiable requirements or design principles of the team. The "Flexible" column describes the kinds of choices that are up to the team's discretion.

TEAM NAME: *Professional Learning Team*

	Fixed	Flexible
Objective • Outcome-based objectives • Process-based objectives	• Plan and/or facilitate "tier 1" professional learning for the faculty, to include 20 hours of PD of after-school time, meaningfully connected to other job-embedded experiences • Build teachers' capacities relative to the priorities of our school improvement plan (changes annually) • Strengthen our own capacities as leaders of adult learning	• How this PD connects to our peer-observation cycles, CPT meetings, and coaching • Whether the team brings in PD leaders from other schools or partners and/or leads sessions themselves • Ideally will help build relationships of respect and personal regard among the whole faculty

Team Composition
• Transparency of selection
• Strategic teaming (matching expertise and dispositions to the task)
	• No more than eight teachers, plus literacy and math coaches
	• Candidates nominated or self-nominated
	• Literacy and math coaches make final selection decision, by interview if necessary
	• Composed of individuals who are
	  » Effective teachers of kids
	  » Interested in strengthening their skills as facilitators and professional learning leaders of adults
	  » Willing to take risks and try new practices
		• Experience leading PD is not necessary
		• Not necessarily staffed by grade-level reps (ideal, but not essential)
		• Open to all teacher stakeholder groups
		• Members are encouraged but not required to participate in district PD on adult learning
		• Principal will join meetings whenever possible and when requested

Key Activities • Decisions • Actions • Dispositional	• Identifying professional growth targets • Designing professional learning activities to involve the whole staff • Communicating PD priorities and plans • Evaluating PD and ensuring continuous improvement	• How often to adjust targets • How they will be monitored/measured • Forms of PD: book groups, seminars, online learning, walk-throughs, video lessons, and so on • How we apply principles of adult learning to our own meetings
Logistics • Meeting duration, frequency, and schedule • Meeting attendance • Meeting roles • Between-meeting work	• Meets twice each month after school for at least one hour • Attendance at all meetings is expected • Two to four hours of work is expected between meetings (reading, preparing, etc.) • Team members will rotate meeting roles	• Team can decide meeting schedule and could agree to meet longer • Team may decide to create subcommittees • Team determines what work must be done between meetings to be prepared for PD sessions

FIGURE 4.2 TEAM DESIGN TOOL continued

	Fixed	Flexible
Support • Time • Skill-building support/feedback • Access (to data, info., key people, etc.) • Compensation	• Members will have two release periods per month to connect with others around PD • Members will receive a copy of two shared texts • The team will have access to school-wide reports of student data • Members will receive a stipend of $1,000	• Members can use the release periods to engage in research, planning, observation, modeling, meeting with coaches, and so on • Additional release time may be requested • Members to have choice in which texts are purchased
Communication • Within the team • From the team • With others engaged in the same leadership functions	• Members will agree to follow school norms for communication, note-taking, and archiving team artifacts for future use • Team will communicate regularly with the faculty about PD exit slip themes and how the team is responding to feedback therein	• Communicating with district curriculum and instruction offices as needed • Communicate resource needs to principal

time, the document sees fewer changes, as the team settles into a routine. Once negotiated in this space, the document serves as a "job description" of sorts for team membership.

Teacher Leadership Through Roles

Some leadership functions will be assumed by individuals in formal roles instead of teams. Too often, when thinking about formal teacher/leader roles, we start by thinking about these leaders' titles or actions instead of what we want them to accomplish. Where these roles are new roles, it's possible instead to design them backward for maximum impact. The next tool can help.

Teacher/leader roles do not influence students directly. It is through teacher/leaders' interactions with other teachers, and the extent to which those interactions influence those teachers' practices, that teacher/leaders have an impact on student learning. The Role Design Tool in Figure 4.3 shows how we might approach planning a new role if we are starting with the end in mind: (1) What are the intended outcomes for students? (2) What would their teachers have to do differently to achieve those outcomes? (3) What kinds of interactions could a teacher/leader have with those teachers in order to facilitate those changes? A blank copy of the Role Design Tool is provided in Appendix A, as well as online.

The Role Design Tool allows leaders who are creating new roles to consider the logic behind those roles. One benefit in designing a role this way is that impact

FIGURE 4.3 ROLE DESIGN TOOL

Plan new roles backward by starting with the Needs Analysis in Part C. Then describe the role in 1–3 sentences (Part B) and, finally, give it a meaningful title (Part A).

A. Role Title:

Math Success Supporter

B. Role Description:

Support teachers in providing effective whole group and targeted small group math instruction as well as to implement a student work exhibition system by providing coaching, data support, research, and other resources.

C. Needs Analysis:

Intended Outcomes Which specific groups of students will be affected? How?	Intended Outputs Which specific teachers will be influenced? How?	Key Tasks or Activities What will the teacher leader do to achieve these results?
Data show that 57% of girls in grades 3–5 are performing below "Proficient" on our end-of-year math assessments, compared with 40% of boys in the same performance level We want to decrease the performance gap between girls and boys and increase the math performance of all upper elementary students. By next year, the percentage of 3rd to 5th grade girls performing below proficient will be cut by two-thirds and the percentage of boys performing below will be cut in half.	Third-fifth grade teachers will provide whole group instruction that supports all students' sense of safety and confidence.	Support teachers to interview students (all genders) to hear their hopes, fears, and expectations about math and to address emerging themes
		Share research and other resources to inform development of an effective response
	Third-fifth grade teachers will provide small group instruction to targeted intervention groups to address skills gaps	Provide data analysis support and intervention resources
		Provide instructional coaching to ensure high-level implementation of intervention strategies
	Third-fifth grade teachers will provide opportunities for students to reflect on and celebrate their own learning successes through student work portfolios and classroom exhibitions.	Support teachers with resources, (e.g. sample portfolios, student reflection templates, etc.)
		Support organization of family and community portfolio exhibition

monitoring is built in. That is, since certain forms of evidence pointed to the need for the role in the first place, over time one simply has to monitor those same forms of evidence for signs of change.

Just as with team agreements, agreements about individual roles should be clarified and shared publicly. Although the "fixed" and "flexible" format used for teams would also work for individuals, it can be useful to have a more traditional job description for specific positions, as it can facilitate recruitment for the role.

The Role Description Template presented in Figure 4.4 has been populated with ideas that illustrate the range of responsibilities that a "grade-level team leader" might take on, enabling users to narrow it down to suit their own purposes. A blank copy of the template is provided in Appendix A and online.

FIGURE 4.4 ROLE DESCRIPTION TEMPLATE

TEACHER LEADERSHIP ROLE DESCRIPTION
Role Title: *Grade-Level Team Leader*
ROLE SUMMARY

Purpose

Provide a description of this role's purpose by identifying the leadership function(s) it addresses and by connecting, where possible, to specific school or district goals.

The grade-level team leader influences the professional capacity and shared instructional expectations of the school through the structures and culture she creates for teachers to learn together and from one another in grade-level teams. The grade-level team leader also influences the quality of schoolwide decision-making; they serve as a member of the school leadership team, responsible for ensuring ongoing, two-way communication between grade-level teachers and the school leadership team.

Role

Provide a brief summary of the primary tasks of this position. Writing this task summary may be easier after defining the responsibilities of the position (below).

The grade-level team leader is responsible for guiding the grade-level team's work and ensuring it is coordinated with school goals. To this end, they lead the grade-level team in pursuing effective data-based inquiry cycles. Results are used at the team level for making curricular decisions, developing instructional responses, and guiding examination of further evidence, including student work. Results are also used at the school level, as the school leadership team will establish schoolwide priorities, plan professional development, and cultivate a professional culture of shared ownership for student learning in the school.

(continued)

FIGURE 4.4 ROLE DESCRIPTION TEMPLATE continued

TEACHER LEADERSHIP ROLE DESCRIPTION

ESSENTIAL RESPONSIBILITIES

List each main area of responsibility and give examples of the types of tasks that those responsibilities might entail. Required duties and deliverables should be described separately using clear and concise language.

Areas of Responsibility

Serve as a grade-level instructional leader. This may include
- Provide leadership in the collection and analysis of data, including student work
- Lead the creation and implementation of grade-level goals
- Ensure the maintenance of effective routines for monitoring student progress
- Lead discussions about and improvement of grade-level curriculum and instruction
- Provide the necessary information, encouragement, and support for team development
- Ensure grade-level team meeting findings and conclusions are communicated with the school leadership team

Serve as a representative of the grade-level team on the school leadership team. This may include
- Collaborate with school leaders and other colleagues to address team, grade-level, and instructional issues
- Collaborate to develop priorities for academic improvement
- Assist in facilitating schoolwide professional development activities
- Act as a liaison between school leaders and teachers to ensure effective communication

Serve as facilitator of grade-level team meetings. This may include
- Schedule and plan team meetings
- Facilitate team meetings and keep team on task
- Ensure communication and follow-through between meetings

Required Duties and Deliverables
- Attend all school leadership team meetings.
- Share access to grade-level team meeting agendas and notes with school leadership team.
- Maintain an updated grade-level calendar of events, projects, and deadlines.

Reports to
School Principal

QUALIFICATIONS

Identify the knowledge, skills, and/or abilities required for the satisfactory performance of the position. Then provide the minimum qualifications for the position, such as work experience, formal training, education, certifications, and/or licensures.

Knowledge, Skills, and Dispositions

Required	Preferred
Collecting and interpreting quantitative and qualitative data Analyzing data with attention to cultural proficiency Monitoring progress and maintaining focus on continuous improvement Building community and shared ownership Managing groups Facilitating dialogue Communication Is collaborative Is reliable	Knowledge of adult learning and development Preparing a team for data use Knowledge of content and grade-level standards Knowledge of group and organizational learning Leading professional learning Systems thinking Is interested in the larger/bigger picture Has a growth mindset Enjoys challenges Possesses courage to take risks Honors all perspectives

FIGURE 4.4 ROLE DESCRIPTION TEMPLATE continued

TEACHER LEADERSHIP ROLE DESCRIPTION

QUALIFICATIONS

Education, Training, and Experience

Must have experience engaging in data-based inquiry (at least at the classroom level).

Must have completed three years of teaching experience.

Must be a teacher with permanent status.

SUPERVISION

Provide a summary of the type of support and evaluation that the grade-level team leader can expect to receive. Also, describe how and when the position will be evaluated.

Support

The principal will ensure that the grade-level team leader has the resources needed to perform the role with quality.

- Time: Teacher leader will have 40 min. of additional release time per week to plan and prepare for weekly grade-level meetings.
- Feedback: Teacher leader will meet monthly with the other grade-level team leaders and the principal to review the "Essential Responsibilities" above, discuss successes and challenges, share role-relevant artifacts, and exchange growth-oriented feedback.
- PD/Training: Principal will provide resources ($50 toward professional books, plus training fees as funds allow) to support the teacher leaders to bolster role-relevant leadership skills.
- Access to data and information: Grade-level team leaders will have access to data systems or timely access to data. Principal will ensure grade-level team leaders have the information they need to perform this role well, including relevant district communications.
- Coordination: Principal will also ensure that the role and responsibilities of the position will be communicated to all individuals with whom the grade-level team leader works and will be included in relevant conversations among others performing the same leadership functions.

Evaluation

In bi-annual meetings, the principal and the grade-level team leader will meet one-on-one to review the teacher leader's list of role responsibilities and the principal's list of supervisory supports. They will also review relevant role artifacts (agendas, minutes, charts, self-reflections, activity logs, etc.) to identify successes and challenges. Within this structure, the grade-level team leader and the school principal will determine whether role expectations are being met, and identify supports needed to address any ongoing challenges.

SELECTION AND LENGTH OF SERVICE

Provide a brief summary of the selection process, and describe the term limits for the role.

- Participants apply by writing a letter of interest that describes evidence of mastery of at least three of the required qualifications of the role (see above) and identifying three things they hope to learn from the role. Applicants meeting the established criteria will be interviewed and considered for the position by the school's administrative team.
- Position reopens for qualified applicants at end of each year. All teachers who have completed three years of teaching will be encouraged to apply. Incumbent may reapply, but after three years of service, the preference is for a rotation of roles.

COMPENSATION

Describe the compensation, if any, for the performance of this role.

- Grade-level team leaders receive a stipend of $1,000 to be paid by the school. In addition, they are relieved of one weekly administrative duty in order to use the time to plan and prepare for team meetings.

The template has several features designed to address common issues with role clarity:

- *Role Summary*. This section lays out the role's purpose. Too often we become so caught up in implementing the work that we forget the original goal. (We're not having grade-level meetings just to have them. If the grade-level team leader is successful, what will the meetings accomplish?) Clarifying the purpose up front also provides a clear guide to return to as the role is renegotiated over time: Do we still feel the tasks and responsibilities are aligned with the purpose? What are we learning from the work that can help us better meet the goals? If the role summary identifies the key leadership functions served by the role (see Figure 3.2), this helps to situate the role in the context of other leadership roles with which this role must be in sync.
- *Essential Responsibilities*. This section clarifies the main areas of responsibility. Many educators make the mistake of trying to list every task for which the teacher leader will be responsible. Most roles require teacher leaders to be creative in how they respond within designated areas of responsibility, so a list of tasks would be impossible. Further, the length of a true list of tasks would overwhelm. At the same time, some job descriptions offer a list of tasks that ends with "other duties to be assigned." This puts no limits on the role, and any teacher leader should be wary of accepting such a vague commitment. This section should describe the main areas of responsibility and can provide examples of the type of tasks they entail. Any required duties and deliverables should be spelled out explicitly.
- *Qualifications*. This section provides an opportunity to distinguish the skills one is expected to bring to the role from the skills one will be expected to develop (with support or on one's own). The skills list in Figure 3.3 can be helpful for identifying the knowledge, skills, and dispositions that are essential for the role. Any skills that are truly *essential* to the role must either be highlighted as selection criteria *or* be built in to the supervision plan, so that teachers will be guaranteed the support to develop those skills. It is important to indicate which skills and qualifications are required and which are preferred.
- *Supervision*. The importance of supervision supports is often overlooked. They are essential because leadership knowledge and skill development is not typically part of a teacher's preparation. Most often, teachers in leadership roles will need to learn the requisite knowledge and skills on the job through supervisory support in the form of direct coaching, peer coaching, financial support for training, or reference to resources. Ideally, the teacher leader will also have

opportunities for evaluation and growth-oriented feedback that allow leadership development to be advanced proactively, and not only when issues arise. This evaluation should be independent; teachers should not be given poor teaching performance evaluation ratings for duties they have taken on beyond their teaching responsibilities.

- *Selection and Length of Service.* Clarifying policies related to the selection process helps to avoid future problems, too. A transparent and meaningful selection process that prioritizes the necessary expertise is essential to the teacher's authority in the role. In addition, having "term limits" is an overlooked necessity with teacher leader roles. If there is no shared understanding of how long the teacher will remain in the role, there is reduced flexibility when other roles or individuals might be a better match.

- *Compensation.* Compensation can take many forms. If the teacher leader doesn't receive a stipend or salary increment, they should receive release time. If the position deserves a written job description with this much thought and length, then it deserves compensation.

Knowing what every team and role is designed to accomplish and being aware of how it will do so is essential to coordinating with those efforts and staying in sync. It is also a solid foundation on which to make better matches between teachers and the formal roles and teams they serve.

As indicated previously, it is recommended to jump in to teacher leadership by identifying roles for teachers before identifying priorities that need attention and assessing the expertise available to address those priorities. Nevertheless, Figure 4.5 lists 50 possible teacher leader roles, provided to expand teacher/leaders' thinking about the great range of teams and roles that teachers currently hold in schools.

Supports for Formal Teams and Roles

Formal teacher leadership teams and roles must be supported by strategic moves of administrators. These supports are important because formally designated roles have a higher level of accountability for both the teacher and the principal, and, in fairness, accountability should be balanced with a commitment to ensure that success is possible. While the strategies for creating a culture for teacher leadership, provided in Figure 4.1, are applicable here, Figure 4.6 presents additional conditions that are particularly important in the context of formal teacher leadership roles. School administrators establishing teams or roles must ask:

FIGURE 4.5 50 TEACHER LEADER ROLES

The roles listed below describe positions through which teachers might influence the quality of teaching and learning beyond their own classrooms. Many roles do so through their impact on instruction, school culture, or the operation of the school as an organization.

Instruction	Culture	Organizational Improvement	All or Other
1. New teacher mentor	17. School climate committee leader/member	26. Grade-level/content team facilitator	37. Professional learning/PD leader
2. Mentor for student teachers	18. Behavior intervention and supports team leader/member	27. Before-/after-school program coordinator	38. Reflective practice/Critical Friends Group (CFG) leader
3. Teacher evaluator/consulting teacher	19. Equity and inclusion team member/leader	28. Summer/vacation school program coordinator	39. Book group leader/member
4. Peer assistance and review (PAR) panelist	20. Student advisory leader/member	29. Grant writer/manager	40. Online network leader
5. Demonstration teacher	21. Student support team leader/member	30. Community partnership liaison	41. Action research investigator
6. Peer observation partner	22. Outreach community coordinator/team member	31. Governing board member/School Site Council (SSC) member	42. Teacher activist/advocate
7. Instructional coach (may be by subject area, instructional approach, or student need)*	23. Sunshine Club coordinator/member	32. School redesign team leader/member	43. Policy fellow
8. Assessment design specialist	24. Family engagement liason*	33. School or program review team leader/member	44. Higher education adjunct/clinical faculty member
9. Data coach/data inquiry leader	25. Faculty senate chair	34. Accreditation team leader/member	45. Teachers' union officer
10. Curriculum developer		35. School committee member	46. Teachers' union building representative
11. Curriculum vertical alignment team leader/member		36. Superintendent's or state teacher advisory council member	47. Professional association leader
12. Professional learning community (PLC) facilitator			48. National Board Certification candidate support provider
13. School instructional leadership team leader/member			49. Educator/Teacher of the Year
14. Instructional technology leader			50. Conference presenter/keynote speaker
15. Intervention team facilitator			
16. Department head			

*For example, TELL Survey (New Teacher Center, n.d.), TNTP Insight Survey (TNTP, n.d.), or 5Essentials survey (Urban Education Institute, n.d.)

FIGURE 4.6 CONDITIONS IMPORTANT FOR THE SUCCESS OF FORMAL TEACHER LEADERSHIP

This table extends the list provided in Figure 4.1 with additional conditions necessary for formal roles.

Condition	Questions for Evaluating This Condition	Sample Strategies for Creating This Condition
A. Clearly Defined Roles	**Does everyone who interacts with your teacher leaders understand what the role is (and is not)?** Be sure that formal teacher leadership responsibilities you assign are clearly defined in a job description and explicitly tied to local goals (e.g., define what the role involves AND what place the role has in the larger reform plan). This should be defined publicly, so that all know what they can and should not expect from the holder of this role. This can also be used as a frame for outcome-based evaluation and should guide growth-oriented feedback.	A1. Create and share publicly the job description; ensure it is discussed prior to assignment A2. Ensure the staff handbook explains the role A3. Clarify in situ (e.g., "As part of her role . . .") A4. Agree on who will do what, then stick to it OR communicate about changes
B. Purposefully Selected Teachers to Hold Those Roles	**How do you match teachers with leadership roles?** Be sure to carefully consider how to make strategic matches between the knowledge and skill set required for the role and the teachers who have the requisite knowledge and skills and who want the role. (This means you need a way to learn what teachers know and can do.)	B1. Use an application process or talk directly to potential teacher leaders so that you learn what they bring to the role and can find out what support they will need to do it well B2. Ensure match process offers two-way preview so that teachers have a clear idea of what they may be getting into B3. Assign (or reappoint) roles all at one time, not one at a time, in order to make the most strategic matches B4. Set term limits, so that there is room to reassign each year, as needed to make better matches
C. Culture of Professional Regard	**Are teachers in your school prepared to follow those you've designated as leaders?** Be sure that your assignments of teacher leaders to roles have some credibility among teachers.	C1. Establish routines that ensure teachers in the school know each other's professional strengths C2. Make decision-making process transparent C3. Consider social capital (who has it and how you can support teachers to build it)
D. Leadership Training	**How do you support teachers to build the leadership (non-instructional) skills they need to be successful in the roles you have assigned to them?** For each role you have assigned, be sure you have also ensured supports for teachers to learn how to do well what they are being asked to do.	D1. Support participation in leadership training programs D2. Encourage participation in cohorts so that teacher leaders can learn from one another's leadership dilemmas D3. Recommend books, articles, and web-based resources on leadership; reserve time to discuss them D4. Be a mentor; take time to reflect together on leadership puzzles and practice

(continued)

FIGURE 4.6 CONDITIONS IMPORTANT FOR THE SUCCESS OF FORMAL TEACHER LEADERSHIP continued

Condition	Questions for Evaluating This Condition	Sample Strategies for Creating This Condition
E. **Time**	**How do you create and safeguard the time teacher leaders need to prepare for and perform their roles effectively?** If teacher leaders are to influence colleagues' instruction, they must have time with colleagues around instruction (observing and discussing it). Be sure they also have time to prepare for the work of the role.	E1. Assign hybrid roles or job-sharing roles (allowing them to teach part time and perform their leadership role part time) E2. Assign extra admin/duty periods to teachers holding a role E3. Compensate teachers for using time outside of school E4. Assign administrative support staff, a sub, or an aide to take on some of the teacher leader's nonprofessional duties E5. Schedule planning periods strategically E6. Protect time that has been allocated for teacher leaders to do the work of the role E7. Provide infrastructure and promote culture for technology solutions to improve efficiency and save time: collaborative work, announcements/information sharing, and meetings
F. **Communication and Feedback Routines**	**How do you maintain ongoing two-way communication with teacher leaders so that they can build and feel a sense of success in the role?*** Be sure there is a routine for regular communication between the teacher leader and the principal, a check-in time to address issues proactively regarding resources needed, political tensions, culture issues, and the like; to get warm and cool feedback on the performance of the role; and to be shown appreciation for work in the role. **Important for retention, especially for under-compensated positions.*	F1. Keep a standing appointment, (e.g., biweekly) to check in F2. Establish routine of revisiting the job description regularly; use it as a framework for goal-setting and growth-oriented feedback F3. Have evidence-based discussions (use meeting notes, surveys/meeting exit slips, etc.) F4. Be a learner yourself; be open to feedback, willing to take risks, fail and learn F5. Do NOT rely on e-mail for this kind of communication
G. **Coordinated Leadership Vision**	**How does your school ensure that teachers are not getting mixed messages from various leaders and that there are no major gaps or redundancies in how leadership is enacted?** Be sure there is a clearly communicated vision about how the leadership actions of multiple individuals will add up to a coherent, positive influence on teaching and learning.	G1. Agree upon and share clear, consistent expectations for quality instruction and quality leadership G2. Co-construct an organizational chart and/or logic model that maps out each individual's role G3. Establish efficient communication routines and regular opportunities to check in on leadership alignment G4. Ensure leadership team (including teacher leaders) engages in leadership learning together and/or has opportunities to (and is expected to) tell each other what they are learning that might be useful to the organization

1. Does everyone who interacts with your teacher leaders understand what the role is (and is not)?
2. How do you match teachers with leadership roles?
3. Are teachers in your school prepared to follow those you've designated as leaders?
4. How do you support teachers to build the leadership skills they need to be successful in the roles you have assigned to them?
5. How do you create and safeguard the time teacher leaders need to prepare for and perform their roles effectively?
6. How do you maintain ongoing two-way communication with teacher leaders so that they can build and feel a sense of success in the role?
7. How does your school ensure that teachers are not getting mixed messages from various leaders and that there are no major gaps or redundancies in how leadership is enacted?

Many of the conditions described in Figure 4.6 can be addressed by having a clear and comprehensive role description (see Figure 4.4).

Coordinating and Communicating

With multiple teams and roles at work, the issue of how all these teacher/leaders will coordinate their efforts becomes paramount. Schools with multiple full-time administrators often have devised systems for sharing the work. When it comes to expanding formal roles to include multiple teachers as leaders, we are less likely to have talked this through.

Shared Mental Models of Co-Performance

Perhaps your school's principal and literacy coach both aim to influence literacy instruction. What is their vision of how they will co-perform leadership in this area? Perhaps one is providing support and the other accountability. Perhaps one will introduce teachers to new ideas and practices, while the other will support teachers with implementation. Or, will they divide the faculty so that each will focus their attention on half of the faculty? There is not one right way to co-perform leadership. The size of the school, staffing patterns, leaders' specialized expertise, and the school's particular priorities are just some of the important factors that shape a school's ideal model.

The activity described in Figure 4.7 is a valuable one for leaders working in the same areas of improvement. The figure introduces a thinking exercise that teacher/leaders can explore together to consider how their leadership influences

FIGURE 4.7 LEADERSHIP CO-PERFORMANCE MODELS

The Leadership Models cards can be used to explore the relationship between two sources of leadership that influence the same leadership function. This can be two individual leaders, two teams, or a team and an individual (e.g., the principal and literacy coach, the instructional leadership team and the literacy team, or the math coach and the math team leader).

1. Examine individually
   a. Print a copy of the Leadership Models cards for each individual or team member.
   b. Allow a few minutes for each to examine the cards on their own.

2. Analyze
   a. What is suggested by each model? Can you think of a real-life example in which leadership is co-performed in this way?
   b. Under what conditions, or in what situations, would certain models be preferable or more appropriate than others?

3. Apply
   a. Have each individual draw a model that depicts their conception of how they currently co-perform leadership with another leader or team.
   b. They can use the cards as models or add their own forms.
   c. They can include additional leaders and annotate the illustration with labels to identify roles and relationships.
   d. Share and compare.

4. Extend
   a. Co-construct a model of how you (as a group) would like to see leadership align.
   b. Identify similarities and differences with the individual models.
   c. Identify what would be required to align leadership in the way you have illustrated.
   d. What would be the likely impact on student learning if you are able to align leadership in this way? The impact on teachers? The impact on administrators?

5. Synthesize
   a. Which elements (e.g., ideas, questions, artifacts) of this experience do we want to retain for our work ahead?
   b. Are there others we might inform or involve directly or indirectly? What next steps immediately come to mind?
   c. What can we commit to?
   d. What do we need to be successful?

6. Follow up
   Set another meeting date to check in on your commitments.

FIGURE 4.7 LEADERSHIP MODEL CARDS continued

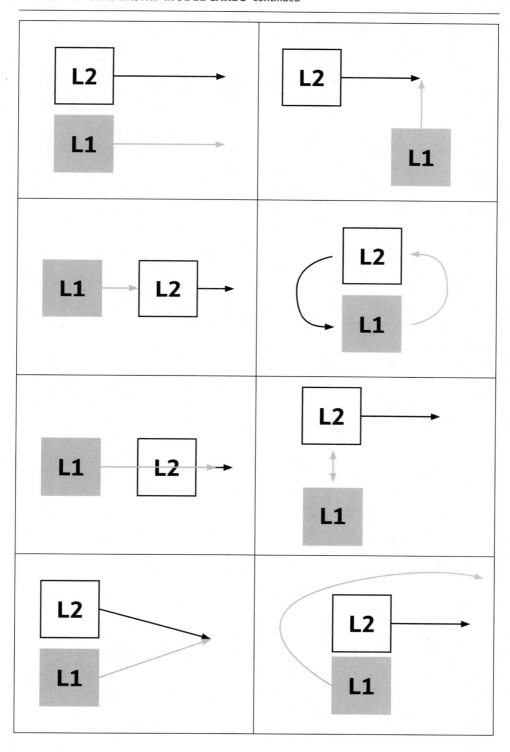

coincide, conflict, or coordinate. It supports them to enter into the conversations needed regarding hidden assumptions about leadership co-performance. Is this a relationship of delegation or partnership? Am I here to reinforce you or to provide an alternative viewpoint? Are you asking or telling me what to do?

Each of the eight leadership co-performance models illustrated in Figure 4.7 suggests the influence of two leaders (or teams). As teacher/leaders collaborate to put words to the relationship they see in each picture, they find themselves listening to how each other thinks about leadership and exploring possibilities they hadn't considered for leadership co-performance. They begin thinking together about the kind of co-performance relationship they would like to see and discussing what this kind of change will require.

For teachers/leaders working within the same leadership function (see Figure 3.2), it is especially important to think about this together. If all leaders share the same assumptions about how roles relate and interact, the roles can be more effective and efficient in carrying out their work.

Another strategy for accomplishing this at the team level is creating metaphor maps (see Figure 4.8). Team members simply work in small groups to create a visual metaphor representing the team's relationship with the school and/or with the other teams in the school. As they do so, assumptions surface about how the team functions, its interactions with other teams, and the fundamental role it plays in the school.

Having a clear, shared sense of everyone's intended role in the co-performance of leadership is important, yet things in schools don't always go as intended. The schedule changes, someone is absent, expected resources are unavailable, and more. Thus, teacher/leaders need to establish structures and routines to ensure they are able to communicate across the work and about the work. This is critical to keeping them in sync.

Communication Routines

It would be ideal if teacher/leaders engaged in co-performance of leadership could read each other's minds. Each would be able to see where the other is headed and contribute their complementary talents to getting us there. When they can't read each other's minds, they can read each other's plans and literally be on the same page. A meeting agenda that is complete with everyone's role spelled out and a clear plan for addressing meeting objectives makes the facilitator's thinking visible and makes it easier for others to effectively follow the facilitator's lead. Further, if members are absent from the meeting, they are able to review what happened, what was decided, and what was learned. Figure 4.9 provides an annotated meeting agenda template. A blank copy of the template is provided in Appendix A, as well as online.

FIGURE 4.8 METAPHOR MAPS

Use this activity to explore the vision of a team's role within the school.

1. Get ready: Divide your team into groups of three.
2. Explain: You have 15 minutes to create a poster that uses a metaphor to represent our team's relationship to the school and the other teams within it. Be prepared to present and explain your poster.
3. Support: Teams will usually spend the first several minutes brainstorming ideas before sketching their ideas out. Encourage this predrawing conversation.
4. Share out: After approximately 15 minutes, each group will take turns explaining its metaphor. At the end of each presentation, ask the other teams to identify what they liked about the metaphor. Ask the presenting team if there are limitations to the metaphor or ways the metaphor is not like our team.
5. Debrief: There is no need to choose a "winner." When all groups have finished, lead a whole-group discussion about (1) common themes across the metaphors and (2) how each metaphor enriches our understanding of our team and its role in the school.

Sample 1

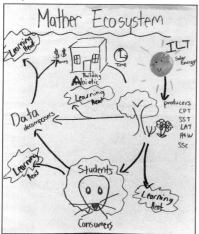

Sample 2

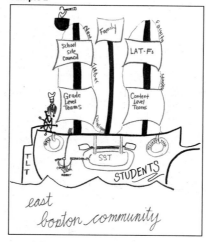

Sample 3

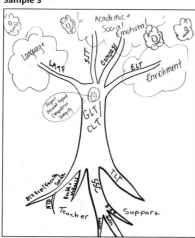

Sample 4

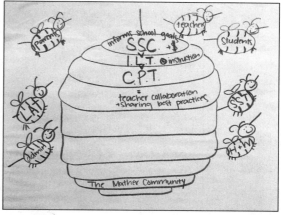

FIGURE 4.9 ANNOTATED MEETING AGENDA TEMPLATE

A structured agenda makes it easier for all to share ownership of the meeting, to take on meeting roles, and to follow through on tasks.

MEETING [#]–DATE

Team Purpose

This may be handed to you or decided by the team. Clarify and copy into the template to remain at the top of the agenda all year.

Meeting Norms	**Meeting Roles**
Develop norms during one of the first three meetings, after the team has had a chance to fully review the team's charge and understand what the work will involve. Copy into the template to remain here all year.	Facilitator: name Notetaker: name Timekeeper: name Norms monitor: name Task collector: name Snack host: name *Link the Roles Rotation Schedule here.*

Meeting Attendance

At the beginning of the meeting, the notetaker will add names or initials of meeting attendees here.

Schedule

Time	Min.	Activity
3:30–3:35	5	**Check in** The facilitator types an icebreaker/energizer question in here. The goal is to bring al voices in the room and build trust (respect and personal regard). **Notes:** The notetaker captures notes in this section if needed.
3:35–3:36	1	**Review objectives for this meeting** Multiple objectives for this meeting were brainstormed at the end of the last meeting. As part of the process of planning this meeting, the facilitator checks in with the principal to determine which are priorities and to learn about any new items (e.g., data review, district visits).
3:36–3:39	3	**Review next steps from previous meeting** This is a chance to check in on completed and outstanding tasks. It is also an opportunity to build trust (integrity), as we acknowledge individuals for following through on commitments. Finally, it leaves space for members to provide any reactions from school teams to last meeting's report. The task collector from the previous meeting would have collected tasks throughou the meeting in a grid like the one below at the end of that agenda. This week's facilitator simply has to copy this "Next Steps" chart from the end of last meeting's agenca and paste it here.

Person Responsible	Task	Anticipated Completion Date
All members	*This table and the text it contains are copied from the end of the previous meeting's agenda.*	

Pause to see if there were any responses or questions from teams about this report

FIGURE 4.9 ANNOTATED MEETING AGENDA TEMPLATE continued

Time	Min.	Activity
3:39–3:40	1	**Review plus (+)/delta (□) summary from previous meeting** This week's facilitator summarizes last week's plus/delta chart with just a few bullets identifying the themes. They might also add a comment here about how last meeting's feedback was used to make this meeting even better. (The responsiveness to others' needs is a way of showing personal regard.) Members review the summary and have a chance to be reminded of meeting elements the team wants to improve.
3:40–4:20	40	**Objective 1** Objective copied here from where it was listed above. **Purpose:** The facilitator frames the conversation by clarifying the purpose and connecting the conversation we're about to have with prior work. (Could be written as an essential question.) **Process:** • The facilitator lays out the key steps in the process they have designed to address this objective (15 minutes). • Sometimes links to relevant docs, sites, or videos are embedded here. • We try to put time markers in lengthy agenda items (15 minutes). This helps the timekeeper keep up with their task. • We try to link any documents that will be necessary for this meeting so that they are easily accessible. This might include readings, data tables, or blank Google Docs in which teams will complete a meeting task. • Sometimes we do a "live write," which is a time-efficient way for everyone to get their ideas out on a discussion topic, question, or reflective prompt (10 minutes). • First everyone just types in at once. <table><tr><td>Member 1</td><td>Members type ideas or question responses here.</td></tr><tr><td>Member 2</td><td>Everyone writes something different . . . usually.</td></tr><tr><td>Member 3</td><td>This chart just fills up with good ideas.</td></tr><tr><td>or</td><td></td></tr><tr><td>Grade 1</td><td>Members can see what others are writing as they write it.</td></tr><tr><td>Grade 2</td><td>Sometimes that sparks a member to write more.</td></tr><tr><td>Grade 3</td><td>We can all refer to this chart later as necessary.</td></tr></table> Then, we review responses and are able to start the discussion at a different place: with a basic idea of what everyone is thinking. **Next steps:** The facilitator leaves one to five minutes to call for a summary of what we just did and to identify next steps (including possibly reporting the summary to other school teams, which could be added to the "Next Steps" list by the task collector). **Notes:** The notetaker captures notes in this section.
4:20 –4:50	30	**Objective 2** A second topic goes here. **Purpose:** **Process:** **Next steps:** **Notes:**

(continued)

FIGURE 4.9 ANNOTATED MEETING AGENDA TEMPLATE continued

Time	Min.	Activity
		Objective 3 Occasionally there is time for a third topic. **Purpose:** **Process:** **Next Steps:** **Notes:**
4:50–4:52	2	**Review next steps from this meeting***

Person Responsible	Task	Anticipated Completion Date
All team members	*What ideas and decisions from this meeting must be reported to other school teams?* We use this first row to capture anything from the meeting that we'd like to report back. Members are in the habit of copying this row into their own CPT agendas.	Next CPT
Task collector	Collects any tasks that have come up in today's meeting here.	April 15
Task collector	Reviews the tasks at the end of the meeting to be sure they captured them all and that we agree on a completion date.	May 15
Task collector	Must be sure to carry over any continuing tasks from last time.	June 15

*Be sure to carry over any continuing tasks from last time.

Notes:

Time	Min.	Activity
4:52–4:55	3	**Assess what worked well and what we want to improve**

+ (What worked well)	Δ (What to improve in future meetings)/questions
• Live write • • •	• Everyone just types in here. • It's useful to pre-populate this area with bullets so that everyone isn't trying to type in the same spot. • •

Norms monitor's reflection: The norms monitor responds to the two questions below while everyone else is busy adding pluses and deltas.
• Which were hard for us today?
• Which helped us to be productive?

Facilitator's reflection: The facilitator reflects on the meeting here while everyone else is busy adding pluses and deltas.
• What was your personal leadership goal?
• What were the tricky parts of this meeting for you as a facilitator?

FIGURE 4.9 ANNOTATED MEETING AGENDA TEMPLATE continued

Time	Min.	Activity
4:55–5:00	5	**Plan agenda for next meeting**

<table>
<tr><td colspan="3"></td></tr>
</table>

Date:		**Location:**

Facilitator: The notetaker of this meeting becomes the facilitator of the next one.

Objectives:
1. Add future agenda items here throughout this meeting as they come up.
2. Peek at the Year-Long Planning Calendar (which may be found at https://goo.gl/TW43hK) to be reminded of what is coming up.
3. There may be more items than can be taken up at the next meeting. Those that aren't addressed can be scheduled for a future meeting via the Year-Long Planning Calendar.
4. The next facilitator will communicate with the principal to prioritize and decide what gets addressed.

Link the **Year-Long Planning Calendar** here.

Another important part of communicating across roles and teams is to do so over time. How will this year's math coach know what last year's team did? As individuals experience their roles, they make decisions, devise new tools and solutions, create templates and systems, and the like. Too often, these individuals' accomplishments move on with them when they do, leaving the organization to start again or to miss out on the opportunity to continue or build on great ideas. Similarly, team membership changes, leaving next year's team to reinvent this year's work. Schools need to be able to capture individuals' and teams' discoveries as part of an institutional knowledge base in order to maximize opportunities for organizational learning. These accomplishments can become organizational assets with the right structures in place.

Whether teacher/leaders are in the classroom full time, part time, or not at all, they are too busy *not* to take advantage of the efficiencies afforded by communication technology. We simply do not have time for the amount of face-to-face contact required to stay in sync across so many leaders. We also don't have time to surf through endless folders of old e-mails and electronic drives looking for the information or documents we need. A good electronic filing system can help. See Figure 4.10 for guidelines.

An efficient electronic filing system also supports co-performance of leadership because it gives all teacher/leaders real-time access to the information they need to do their work. If I want to take on a task, but I need to ask others for the drafts, lists, and instructions to make it happen, it might be easier for those others to do it. Further, my interest will be dampened if I have to ask the "keeper of the keys." By contrast, it is empowering to be trusted with access to our school's shared

FIGURE 4.10   SHARED FILING CABINET

The following guidelines can be used to support your school to maintain an electronic filing cabinet such as GoogleDrive or Dropbox to maximize organizational learning and support leaders to stay in sync.

To be useful to all throughout the organization, the electronic filing system should

- Be organized by meaningful categories and subcategories
  » Creating meaningful categories and subcategories of an electronic filing system is much more than a clerical task. How we organize our files can shape and unify our thinking about our work. It can help us develop a common language and shared understandings. As we use them, our understanding of the categories will deepen.

- Accommodate all types of resources: docs, links, video, and the like
  » Paper docs should be scanned.
  » Electronic records and docs should be linked in case updates are made at the source. They should also be downloaded with the date in case the link becomes broken.

- Be easy to add to from any device by any user
  » Multiple options, including e-mail.
  » Consider security of sensitive information.

- Have clear labeling conventions
  » Controlled vocabulary helps others to know where to look and how to add to it.
  » Use no more than eight words (always fewer than 260 characters; limit for Windows OS).
  » The first word is important because the computer will default to organizing alphabetically by first word (you might want this to be the date, project name, resource type, and so forth).
  » Include document date or version number where relevant to avoid versioning issues.
  » Similar types of files should have similar naming structure.

- Be uncluttered
  » Final versions
    - Do *not* use the word "final" since you never really know if there will be another version. Instead use "archive" + date tag.
    - Save a pdf version of the file, if possible, so that changes won't be made.
    - Some filing systems allow you to tag or star docs. Use these to mark the final versions, which you will want to access easily.
  » Draft versions
    - Include date in the file name of drafts.
    - Keep earlier drafts in a subfolder labeled "drafts"; when the project is complete, delete it.
  » Temporary files
    - Add "temp" to file names of files that are temporary and can later be erased, so as not to clutter the folders.

- Avoid security concerns
  » Are there certain files only some people should access?
  » Do all need permission to add? To delete or move files? To share them?

- Be available at all times
  » How will you access cloud-based files when the Internet is unavailable?
  » Back up all files

brain, to be someone who has both the discretion to draw upon it to improve our school and the responsibility to contribute to it.

Such a system does not replace important face-to-face conversations; it simply allows the precious few minutes available for face-to-face conversation to be focused on action and reflection.

By developing a logical and efficient electronic filing system, an organization can empower individuals to be both producers and consumers of the organization's knowledge base. They will easily be able to access the information they need to do their work well, and they will be able to share ideas, innovations, and resources that they have discovered through their own professional practice. Most important, documenting what we know and do in shared file cabinets ensures that we have access to the information we need to stay in sync.

This chapter described scenarios in which principals are extending autonomy of teams, teachers are stepping up to fill new roles, and school teams are sharing access to their files. We don't typically see educators willing to make themselves this vulnerable to each other. Under what conditions would teacher/leaders take these risks? They might if they trust each other. Trust is the subject of the next chapter.

A RETURN TO WESTLUND K-8 SCHOOL

The Climate and Culture Team at Westlund School had grown excited about the ideas it had generated to encourage grade-level teams to more meaningfully engage parents as partners in their children's education, and they stood ready to support implementation. Yet they did not predict the push-back they got from some colleagues, least of all from the new family engagement coordinator. After taking a step back, they began to recognize coordination and communication issues that were the root of their problem. They needed to better understand what their responsibility was and the extent of their authority as a team, especially in relation to other roles. This is something the school administrators had not clarified for themselves either, and they committed to working it out together.

The principal joined the next Climate and Culture Team meeting, and together they negotiated what was "fixed" and what could be "flexible" with regard to the team's responsibilities (see Figure 4.2). The team, for example, did not have the authority to empower another team to change a long-standing tradition in the school like Math Night, but they did develop a process by which changes could be discussed. Once the team had a clearer idea of its charge, it wanted to explore the place of the team in the context of other roles and teams using the metaphor maps activity in Figure 4.8. Before they could do this, however, they needed to better understand other key teams and roles in the school, and particularly the new family engagement coordinator position. The principal worked with the new coordinator to establish a role description (see Figure 4.4) and collaborated with other teams to establish their own team designs (see Figure 4.2). These were shared with the full faculty so that there would be clear expectations all around about what each role and team did and did not entail. With that information, the Climate and Culture Team was able to coordinate plans with other efforts in the building and to collaborate with the family engagement team in a way that would allow them to complement one another's work.

In the process, they recognized how important communication would be between the two entities. They agreed that the coordinator would join Climate and Culture Team meetings whenever possible, and when she couldn't, she committed to reviewing the notes in the online agenda (see Figure 4.9) to which she had access. In fact, she found that she could type questions or announcements right into the agenda, which helped her to stay in sync. Going forward, the team also committed to regular check-ins about how leadership of family engagement is shared (see Figure 4.7) and to new norms for documenting and archiving their work (see Figure 4.10) so that the school could build on these successes instead of continually reinventing the wheel.

Reflection

1. Review your responses to the context questions at the beginning of this chapter. What new reflections do you have, and what possibilities for action do you see?
2. How might the ideas and strategies from this chapter help teacher/leaders in your school to co-perform leadership more skillfully?

Strengthening Trust

IN YOUR CONTEXT...

- In what ways does lack of trust get in the way of leading in sync?
- What do educators believe about how trust is built?
- How do teacher/leaders view their role in building trust?

The many individuals who work in a single school bring different perspectives and experiences that shape their diverse opinions about how the school should improve. Under what conditions would they come together around a shared vision powerful enough to push the school forward? For what reason might they be willing to coordinate their efforts in shared leadership? The key is trust.

LARSON HIGH SCHOOL

By all accounts, Larson High School is a great place to work. Teachers meet for happy hour on the last Friday of each month, they have a rockin' holiday party each December, and they have many internal jokes and routines that keep them laughing together. Teacher retention is high, and vacancies are easy to fill. When new members do join the faculty, they are surrounded by offers to help with classroom set-up, finding supplies, and learning school policies.

Within team meetings, teachers like to share stories of funny classroom capers and important news about the students they have in common. They also occasionally share strategies that worked well, exchange instructional tools they've adapted, and collaborate on planning events. At the suggestion of one team member, they even created a parent communication log template together.

In September, a new instructional coach was added to the faculty to help reverse a new downward trend after years of moderately high but stagnant achievement scores. After joining team meetings for a month, she visited classrooms and discovered that some teachers were struggling with challenges that others had the expertise to meet; no one was using the parent communication log they had created together; and her efforts to suggest new strategies were often met with resistance, as some faculty members preferred doing what was familiar instead of trying something new, and others resisted taking advice from this unknown "newbie."

Most schools are cordial workplaces, which makes sense, because educators tend to be nice people. But nice people don't always want to make waves. At the same time, schools are in the business of improvement and improvement is change, which is inherently uncomfortable. Most of us would rather keep doing what we're doing than change, especially when we're unsure about what the change will look like and what part we're expected to play in the change. If we're going to succeed in this work, we have to cultivate a climate that allows us to be comfortable with discomfort. We can't learn from each other, solve previously unsolved problems, or come close to achieving higher hopes for our schools without taking risks.

Under what conditions might I risk my autonomy and agree to work with you? I might do it if I trust you. Under what conditions might you bother to go out of your way to help me improve? Trust plays into your decision.

Trust is essential to establishing the kind of culture in which all teacher/leaders are ready and willing to sync their efforts and push for real improvement. This chapter discusses how teacher/leaders can foster development of trust throughout their school. They must (1) recognize what trust is and what makes it so complex; (2) understand how trust is built; and (3) be able to analyze, diagnose, and create conditions for greater trust-building.

What Is Trust?

Trust is *one's willingness to make oneself vulnerable based on the expectation that the other will act appropriately* (Tschannen-Moran, 2014). Schools that want to improve require vulnerability, because education is an uncertain enterprise. Teaching and learning are such complex processes that we can never really know if X will cause Y. Yet the urgency is so great that we have to try something, and the task is so large that we must work together. Do we trust each other enough to take the risks needed to improve?

Trust and School Improvement

The essential relationship of trust to school improvement has been documented extensively in research. It has been seen to predict which schools make and sustain the greatest gains (Bryk & Schneider, 2002). It has been associated with student achievement gains across all grade levels (Goddard, Tschannen-Moran, & Hoy, 2001; Tschannen-Moran, 2004), as well as across socioeconomic statuses (Adams & Forsyth, 2013; Hoy & Tschannen-Moran, 1999). Studies on the impact of trusting relationships in schools are consistent: whether teacher-to-teacher, teacher-to-student, or teacher-to-family, trust matters (Tschannen-Moran, 2014).

Trust fuels engagement. I'm willing to do my part, but only if I trust that you are going to step up and do yours. Trust makes us willing to engage and, with each successful engagement, I see less risk in engaging again. Soon we're engaging willingly, and others may find it contagious.

Trust drives productivity. Our collective engagement, built on trust, makes us feel accountable to ourselves and each other in ways that push us to put our money where our mouths are. When I see you doing your part, I'm feeling accountable to do mine and to do it well. We begin to trust in our collective ability to produce results.

Most important, *trust enables inspiration.* Trust encourages us to aspire to things we might not have dared and allows us to see new possibilities. This is because once we develop trust in our ability to engage productively together on known goals, we become inspired to consider what else might be possible and to think creatively about new goals. (See Figure 5.1.)

It's nice if teachers like each other. But educators liking each other doesn't guarantee that teachers will take the risks necessary to change teaching practice, to take the initiative to push on one another's thinking, or to challenge each other to consider the impact of their instructional decisions on student learning. Every teacher can lead in these ways, but they need to truly trust each other. They need to trust and be trusted by school administrators too. In many schools, trust is built over time through chance encounters among the staff. I argue that since trust is essential to strong schools, students can't wait. Teacher/leaders must be more deliberate about helping colleagues to develop trust.

To understand how trust is built, it is helpful to recognize two important reasons why trust is so complicated—and too often elusive—in schools. The first is that trust is role-relevant, yet in schools we often lack role clarity. The second is

FIGURE 5.1 ENGAGEMENT, PRODUCTIVITY, AND INSPIRATION

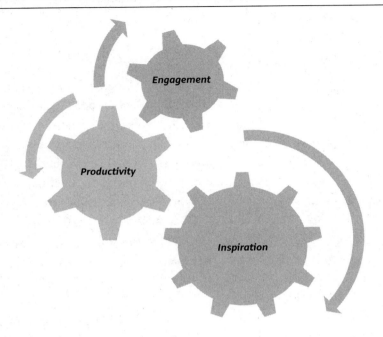

that trust is multidimensional, and in schools when we only have some types of trust, we often fake the others and end up feeling betrayed. These characteristics of trust do make trust complicated, but understanding them can enable us to strategically avoid the pitfalls and succeed in strengthening trust.

Roles and Trust

The first reason trust is complicated is that it is role-relevant. My expectations and determinations about whether another is acting appropriately are tied to what I believe their role is. I trust my husband. But when my 2004 Honda Civic needed a new transmission, I didn't ask him to fix it; I took it to a mechanic. Further, I trusted the mechanic to charge me whatever she wanted, and I trusted her work enough to allow my daughter to drive across the country in that car. If I had tried to tell the mechanic about the many wonderful adventures I'd had in that car, how poignant it felt to pass the car on to my daughter, and about my concern for my daughter's safety on her cross-country trip, the mechanic likely would have snubbed me. Based on her role as a mechanic, it would have been unreasonable for me to expect her to listen. It's not what she expects of me in my role as a client. Instead, my husband got an earful of stories and heard my fears about the trip. Appropriate to his role, he listened, reminded me of a few Honda capers I'd forgotten, and even added some new fears. The role expectations of a mechanic and of a spouse vary across contexts and cultures, but generally people enter into such relationships knowing what to expect.

These roles are a bit more clear-cut than those in schools. That is because educators and family members come from a variety of backgrounds and schooling experiences themselves, bringing a wide range of expectations about the roles of the teacher, the principal, the family member, and the student. We don't necessarily have the same expectations of each other's roles. As a parent approaching a family-teacher conference, should I bring concerns about my ability to help my child with math homework? Or about my child's mental health? As a teacher who sees a colleague struggling with a student in the hallway, am I expected to offer advice or assistance, or to avert my eyes? As a teacher with an idea about how to improve the system we use for tracking benchmark data, is it my role to share that idea with the teacher leader who created it or to keep my mouth shut as a show of support to this colleague who has leadership aspirations? As a principal attending teacher-led content meetings, should I ask a clarifying question when there is something about the content I do not understand, or might that be perceived as challenging the teacher leaders' knowledge and clarity?

When it comes to teacher leadership, the opportunities for miscommunication are especially abundant because of often-unspoken assumptions about teacher leadership. Teacher leadership is understood and enacted differently across different schools, departments, and teams, yet few locales take time to define it explicitly. The tools in Chapter 3 can help you to do so.

Four Types of Trust

The second reason trust is so complicated in schools is that role-relevant trust or "relational trust" has multiple dimensions. Bryk and Schneider's (2002) important work studying school improvement in Chicago lays out four dimensions to relational trust. Since then, others have teased out additional ways of thinking about the different types of trust (e.g., Tschannen-Moran, 2014). What's important about the multiple dimensions of trust is not the number of types. Instead, it's the attention this view of trust draws to the complicated calculus we are making every time we wrestle with the question, "Why should I make myself vulnerable here?" If we can be more conscious of the variations within trust, we can understand the ways people are thinking about this question, and we can take steps that help them choose to trust.

Let's first explore Bryk and Schneider's four types of trust: respect, personal regard, competence, and integrity. To increase your attention to the types of trust that are at play in a relationship, you might ask yourself the following questions:

1. *Do I trust that you will hear and value what I have to say in the context of our role relationship?* If so, I trust you to *respect* me, and I am likely to honor that by showing the same respect to you. I don't expect you to agree with me, but I trust that any expectations I have of feeling heard by you will be met. I trust my mechanic to respect me, because she perfectly meets my role-based expectations that she will value the description I give her about what is wrong with my car, and I don't expect more than that. Sometimes teachers do not feel respected in their schools because they expect principals to value what they have to say about curricular choices, programming decisions, or resource allocation. In fact, some principals do not *expect* teachers to expect this, or if they do, they may not effectively communicate whether or not this is how they view the teacher's role.

2. *Do I trust that you will take actions that have my best interests at heart, even when those actions extend beyond role obligations?* If so, I trust you to have *personal regard,* and I am likely to show my appreciation by reciprocating. My mechanic knew I needed the car in time for my daughter to start her cross-country trip on Friday. Could I get the car by Thursday? The timing would be tight. She'd have to work later than usual, and she'd have to prioritize the job in front of another in her queue. She's willing to put herself out there for me, and I've put myself out there for her by recommending her to new neighbors. After repeated interactions had established a relationship of respect, we had developed personal regard. Teachers have multiple opportunities to extend respect and develop personal regard with each other, as we're constantly going beyond our role obligations to help each other throughout the day: watching another's class, switching bus duties, lending supplies, and so on. Personal regard is complicated when it comes to teachers in leadership roles. Since such roles are commonly undefined, a teacher leader may feel she is going beyond role obligations, while others don't perceive it as such, leaving her to feel her efforts are unappreciated.

3. *Do I trust that you have the capacity to perform your role well?* If so, I trust you to have *competence,* and I will feel increased accountability for the same. I certainly trusted my mechanic to fix the car competently. I might have saved some money and time if I had removed the old transmission myself and just had her put in the new one. This is something I wouldn't trust myself to do. Part of being trustworthy involves being honest about expectations, which may involve declining responsibilities I do not have the skills to fulfill. In schools with teachers in leadership roles, if different leaders have contrasting ideas about what it looks like to do the work at a competent level, someone may feel another has fallen short, that there has been a breach in trust. In fact, some teachers expect to be able to count on school and district leaders to support them in strengthening

the leadership capacity they need for their roles and feel let down if the support is lacking or is not done well.

4. *Do I trust that you will follow through on what you say and are expected to do by virtue of your role?* If so, I trust you to have *integrity* and will likely put pressure on myself to meet my commitments as well. My mechanic did not have to promise the car would be ready by Thursday, but she did and now I am counting on it. I am counting on her, too, to have the integrity not to take any shortcuts or charge me an unfair price. I wouldn't honestly know if she did; it is a matter of trust. If Thursday comes and the car is not ready, I'll trust that she did her best to make the deadline and that something got in the way. As for me, I know what my part is, and I am committed to doing it: I'll bring the car to her on time, and when the car is ready, I'll make sure the bill is paid. It's hard to follow through on something you didn't know you were expected to do. Today, with the proliferation of undefined leadership roles for teachers, unspoken expectations increase the likelihood that feelings of frustration or even betrayal will result when assumed expectations are unfulfilled.

FOUR TYPES OF TRUST

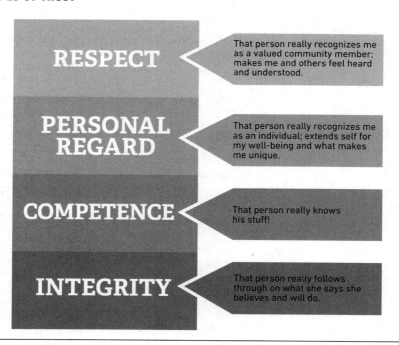

RESPECT — That person really recognizes me as a valued community member; makes me and others feel heard and understood.

PERSONAL REGARD — That person really recognizes me as an individual; extends self for my well-being and what makes me unique.

COMPETENCE — That person really knows his stuff!

INTEGRITY — That person really follows through on what she says she believes and will do.

It's worth taking time to reflect on how these four types of trust play out within different teams and throughout a school. Figure 5.2 offers a resource for deepening understanding and discussing these four types of trust with colleagues. The Types

FIGURE 5.2 TYPES OF TRUST CARDS

RESPECT

Do I trust that you will hear and value what I have to say in the context of our role relationship?

To respect others is to make them feel that you value their qualities, feelings, or abilities. We feel respected when we feel heard and understood, but we don't expect to share everything with all people. Respect is a key aspect of relational trust, because we bring expectations about what we feel we can share with people and what we expect them to listen to based on our understanding of their role.

Relational trust is grounded in the social respect that comes from the kinds of social discourse that take place across the school community. Respectful exchanges are marked by genuinely listening to what each person has to say and by taking these views into account in subsequent actions. Even when people disagree, individuals can still feel valued if others respect their opinions.

Without interpersonal respect, social exchanges may cease. People typically avoid demeaning situations if they can. When they don't have this option, sustained conflict may erupt. Such a situation existed at Ridgeway Elementary School, where interactions among parent leaders and professional staff got in the way of needed reforms. For example, parent and community leaders pressed school staff to implement a "respect program toward students," which included written standards for how adults should talk to students, guidelines to encourage increased sensitivity on the part of school professionals to the ethnic and cultural backgrounds of students, and procedures for handling student misconduct that refrained from punitive and demeaning adult behavior. But little of this same respect was evident in the social interactions among the adults. Parents and community leaders offered rude personal criticism of school staff with little recognition that their behavior was the exact opposite of the behavior that they desired to foster in the students (Bryk & Schneider, 2003).

PERSONAL REGARD

Do I trust that you will take actions that have my best interests at heart, even when those actions extend beyond role obligations?

To have regard for others is to show attention or concern for them. We show regard for others through actions that demonstrate we have taken our knowledge of them into consideration. By virtue of their function, schools are places of attention and concern. We expect a certain regard from each other as a function of our roles as teacher, principal, parent, student, and so on. Personal regard often involves going beyond what we expect from obligatory role responsibilities to do what's best for another. We are feeling personal regard when we say to someone, "You didn't have to do that, but I'm glad you did!"

Personal regard represents another important criterion in determining how individuals discern trust. Such regard springs from the willingness of participants to extend themselves beyond the formal requirements of a job definition or a union contract. The actions of the principal at another of our case study sites, Holiday Elementary School, offer strong testimony. Almost every parent and teacher we spoke with at this school commented effusively about the principal's personal style, his openness to others, and his willingness to reach out to parents, teachers, and students. His efforts helped cultivate a climate in which such regard became the norm across the school community. This climate, in turn, was a major factor in the high level of relational trust found in this most unexpected place—a 100 percent low-income, African American population in a school serving a public housing project, with a white, male principal (Bryk & Schneider, 2003).

FIGURE 5.2 TYPES OF TRUST CARDS continued

COMPETENCE

Do I trust that you have the capacity to perform your role well?

Competence is the ability to do something well. Our determinations about what we expect people to be able to do well depend on their role. Parents don't expect teachers to be able to fix a car engine, and we don't expect parents to perform surgery. A key component, then, of relational trust is being able to trust that others will have competence in core role responsibilities. This is easier when there are clear, shared expectations of what the role responsibilities are.

School community members want their interactions with others to produce desired outcomes. This attainment depends, in large measure, on others' role competence. For example, parents depend on the professional ethics and skills of school staff for their children's welfare and learning. Teachers want supportive work conditions for their practice, which depends on the capacity of the school principal to fairly, effectively, and efficiently manage basic school operations. School administrators value good community relations, but achieving this objective requires concerted effort from all school staff. Instances of negligence or incompetence, if allowed to persist, undermine trust. This was a major factor in the negative parent-school relations at Ridgeway, where some clearly incompetent and uncaring teachers were nonetheless allowed to continue to practice (Bryk & Schneider, 2003).

INTEGRITY

Do I trust that you will follow through on what you say and are expected to do by virtue of your role?

Deeds and words align when one has personal integrity. Not only do we trust people with personal integrity to do what they say they will do, but further, their actions are predictable once we become familiar with the values and principles that guide their decisions. Those values and principles may also be shaped by expectations and obligations of their roles.

Perceptions about personal integrity also shape individuals' discernment that trust exists. The first question that we ask is whether we can trust others to keep their word. Integrity also demands that a moral-ethical perspective guides one's work. Although conflicts frequently arise among competing individual interests within a school community, a commitment to the education and welfare of children must remain the primary concern.

The principal's actions at Ridgeway offer a compelling example of how a perceived lack of commitment to students' welfare can undermine trust. Although members of the school community viewed this principal as a caring person, no one was sure where he stood on a number of internal school conflicts. When concerns surfaced about problematic teachers, he chose an approach sensitive to the particular adults involved. He visited their classrooms and demonstrated lessons, hoping that the teachers would adopt new techniques. When the teachers did not improve, however, he dropped the initiative and did not change the situation. In the end, no one interpreted his action as directed toward the best interests of the students, and these events further exacerbated the distrust across the school community (Bryk & Schneider, 2003).

FIGURE 5.3 TYPES OF TRUST CARDS—EXPLORATION

Your decisions about how to explore the four types of trust will be shaped by various factors, from the group's current feelings about trust (or lack of trust), to the roles of the colleagues involved, to the number of people involved, to how much time you have. Adapt this activity to suit your team's needs.

(Requires 10–20 minutes)
1. Form groups of four to seven people and provide at least one set of cards to each group.
2. Invite group members to take turns reading the cards aloud. Discuss similarities and distinctions across the four types of trust.
3. Discuss one or more of the following questions:
   - Consider teams you have been on in the past (professionally or personally). What is it like when one or two types of trust are absent?
   - Do some types of trust depend on others? What relationships do they have to each other?
   - What does it take to strengthen each type of trust?

Variation for large groups (requires 20–40 minutes and eight or more people)
Organize this activity as a jigsaw: Divide members into four groups and assign each group one type of trust to study and discuss. Then re-form new teams that include representatives of each type of trust, and extend the conversation. Wrap up by inviting teams to report out ideas that are interesting or important, including implications for practice.

Pre-Reading Possibility
Provide copies of "Trust in Schools: A Core Resource for Reform" (Bryk & Schneider, 2003), the article—https://goo.gl/GFmGve—from which the passages on the cards were excerpted. Discuss using a text-based protocol.

Extension Opportunity
Think of a team that you have been on in the past in which trust was either very strong or very weak. What influenced your decision about whether or not to trust?

of Trust Cards can be used or adapted in a variety of ways, including those suggested in Figure 5.3.

Each of these types of trust is essential for teacher/leaders to feel confident about the give-and-take needed to stay in sync. When we are leading together, we have to compromise and communicate in ways that challenge us, and in ways we wouldn't have to if we just claimed the authority to lead alone. If I distrust that other leaders respect me, I will withhold my opinions, including the constructive feedback that our school most needs to grow. If I feel other leaders have no personal regard for me, I will feel my talents are overlooked or taken for granted, and I will resist extending myself for the school. If I feel they doubt my competence or integrity, or if I doubt theirs, we will be fearful of taking on any meaningful work together. To invest myself fully in the hard work our school needs us to do together, I need to know where my fellow leaders and I stand with regard to trust. To do this, it is helpful to understand how trust develops.

How Trust Is Built

The development of trust is complicated by its four component parts. Each type of trust has its own appropriate strategy. Understanding the distinctions between them and the dynamic relationship among them is essential for establishing a trusting and productive culture that capitalizes on all of them.

Building Trust for Better Schools introduces a "Process Model for Building Trust in Schools" (see Figure 5.4) that can help us to do just that (Kochanek, 2005). The model, which uses the four types of trust as building blocks, is drawn from qualitative studies of schools in which an increase in student achievement was associated with an increase in trust. That is, it is focused not on the kind of trust that makes schools a comfortable place to work, but rather on the kind of trust that allows colleagues to safely push each other out of their comfort zones and into higher levels of learning and performance. That kind of trust is an indispensable resource for school improvement and reform.

FIGURE 5.4 PROCESS MODEL FOR BUILDING TRUST IN SCHOOLS

The growth of trust is the result of positive discernments we make about the four types of trust. We make positive discernments about competence and integrity through repeated successful high-risk interactions. We make positive discernments about respect and personal regard through repeated successful low-risk interactions. The more we have successful exchanges, the more we want to have them. Positive conditions set the stage by easing our vulnerabilities.

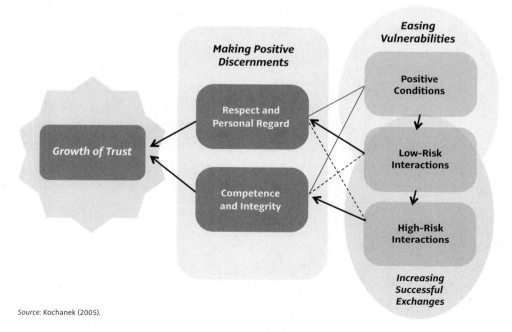

Source: Kochanek (2005).

The Growth of Trust

The model in Figure 5.4 represents the growth of trust as a direct result of positive discernments that educators make about the four types of trust. Trust is a choice. Each time we choose to make ourselves vulnerable—whether by being the first to wave hello in the parking lot or by agreeing to collaborate with a colleague to design new common assessments—we initiate an exchange that informs future decisions about whether to trust like that again. The person may wave back or turn away. The colleague may share the assessment design work and possibly teach you something new in the process or leave you with the lion's share of the work. The more we take risks, the more information we have about whether to trust the other to respect us, to have personal regard, to be competent, and to have integrity. Positive discernments lead to increasing successful exchanges, and negative discernments lead us to avoid taking future risks. In this way, trust is either strengthened or stunted.

How does this cycle get started? High-risk interactions are needed to build positive discernments about competence and integrity. But, most people will not engage authentically in high-risk interactions until they have first established respect and personal regard through low-risk interaction. And, people's willingness to engage in either requires underlying positive conditions. Trust is always a choice. This process model helps us to see how the gradual easing of vulnerabilities can lead to the growth of trust.

The model explains why we are unlikely to agree to design common assessments with someone with whom we haven't already had some interaction. Designing strong common assessments requires time and effort, and my willingness to invest both of these is influenced by my willingness to make myself vulnerable. What if we don't share the same values about what should be assessed? What if I have to compromise my standards? Do I trust that my colleague knows how to do this? Will I get stuck doing most of the work? Designing common assessments is a high-risk activity, as it could consume my time and effort, replace systems with which I am already comfortable, result in tools that are less useful to me, and/ or take up more instructional time. It could potentially have a greater cost than benefit for me and my students. With little knowledge of my colleague, it's hardly worth the risk.

But what if I do know that my colleague and I share the same values and high standards? What if prior exchanges have shown me that my colleague is knowledgeable about designing assessments and is an effective collaborator and a diligent work partner? I might learn something exciting and my students' learning might get a real boost. There's still a high risk, but there's reason to believe that if I ease my vulnerabilities, the reward will be worth the risk. When educators work along-side each other in high-risk exchanges, such as collaborative planning, curriculum development, designing student interventions, or grant writing, we learn the truth about each other's strengths and work ethic. Repeated successful exchanges allow us to build confidence that we can trust in one another's competence and integrity and to build trust. This trust, in turn, allows us to be productive together, enables us to leverage one another's strengths, pushes us to be creative beyond what we could have imagined alone, and makes us want more.

Similarly, most people will not willingly jump into high-risk activities with colleagues without first evaluating how low-risk activities with those same colleagues have gone. Repeated, positive low-risk exchanges help us to build feelings of respect and personal regard and allow us to consider opening ourselves up for high-risk exchanges.

During your first week at a new school, you may make the low-risk choice to wave to someone across the parking lot. If that goes well, you may share a positive observation about last week's successful school assembly, which establishes a connection on common ground and builds respect. You may even compliment your colleague's students' performance within the assembly, a move that acknowledges your colleague's individual effort and signifies personal regard. You've noticed something about this person. They noticed that you noticed. Maybe you're a good match to work together on something. Low-risk exchanges will never push the school forward, but they are essential to creating a climate of readiness for the high-risk exchanges that can. They also build mutual accountability: I will be less likely to let myself let you down after we have built a foundation of low-risk trust.

Use the examples of low- and high-risk interactions among teachers in Figure 5.5 to consider what low- and high-risk interactions between teachers and administrators might look like.

Underlying Conditions of Trust

Educators' decisions to initiate or engage in risky exchanges in the first place are shaped by underlying conditions (C1 in Figure 5.4). Some people are more predisposed to trust; others have had prior experiences in life that make it challenging for them to do so. People often trust those with whom they perceive similarity, whether by race, culture, gender, or perhaps because they've chosen the same shirt to wear, car to drive, or school for their children. Many people are inclined to trust others based on reputation, social status, or hierarchy, but some are skeptical for these same reasons. The underlying conditions affecting trust are subjective. Even mood can affect one's inclination to trust.

FIGURE 5.5 EXAMPLES OF LOW- AND HIGH-RISK INTERACTIONS

Low-Risk Interactions	High-Risk Interactions
Evidence that teachers have made positive discernments about respect and personal regard	*Evidence that teachers have made positive discernments about competence and integrity*
• Teachers take time to greet each other in the morning. • Teachers inquire about each other's weekend on Monday morning. • Teachers know (or know stories about) each other's families, and possibly spend time together outside of school. • Teachers do simple favors for each other (e.g., making coffee, photocopying resources). • There is a social gathering (e.g., team happy hour, staff party) once or twice a year. • Teachers eat lunch together and discuss personal lives. • Teachers know each other's students. • Teachers are familiar with each other's values and views. • Teachers agree with each other in faculty meetings. • Teachers tell each other about a successful encounter with a student. • Teachers are willing to share a resource or lesson plan with another teacher. • Teachers attend workshops together.	• Teachers participate actively in collaborative problem solving during meetings. • Teachers agree to participate in action teams to carry out decisions made by the group. • Teachers express divergent professional views and challenging dilemmas at team/faculty meetings. • Teachers troubleshoot with colleagues to address challenges of managing classroom behavior. • Teachers co-teach, observe, and model for each other; provide each other with feedback. • Teachers feel ownership of all students in the school. • Teachers appreciate conversations that raise differing views, opinions, and values. • Teachers have difficult conversations with colleagues about instructional gaps revealed by student data. • Teachers tell each other about unsuccessful encounters with students, seeking professional opinion. • Teachers collaborate to coordinate their instructional strategies/curriculum within and across grade levels. • Teachers apply for grants together.

Where there are underlying positive conditions, educators are more inclined to connect with each other. As they begin to take small risks, possibly even to share their best lessons and student work with each other, they may pick up good ideas from one another, feel validated about the work they've done, and appreciate each other's efforts. Over time, they are likely to develop respect and personal regard and to be willing to take greater risks. Yet it is not until teachers share their worst lessons and most significant student challenges at team meetings that it becomes possible to reflect together and revise lessons in ways that elevate everyone's practice and to collaboratively problem solve new approaches to student challenges in ways that serve the neediest students. Now the school can really improve.

If we leave trust to chance, faculty members in a school may eventually bump into each other enough to discover that they have some shared values, and over time they might inadvertently discover each other's strengths, but if school improvement depends on it, why not take strategic action to help the discovery process along? The ability of a leadership team, a grade-level team, or even a whole faculty to stay in sync depends on trust. Therefore, teacher/leaders at all levels must share some responsibility for turning these possibilities into probabilities.

Sharing Responsibility for Trust

Teacher/leaders must not overlook the critical role they play in a school's culture of trust. There are many simple things they can do to share responsibility for strengthening trust among themselves as formal leaders, and throughout the whole faculty in informal ways. A first step is to establish positive conditions for trust. Then teacher/leaders can assess the types of trust in place and take deliberate steps to strengthen them.

Establishing Positive Conditions for Trust

Some of the underlying conditions that affect trust are within teacher/leaders' control, and some are not. If someone has experienced a grave breach of trust, it will be hard for that person to trust others. Yet, teacher/leaders are not powerless to influence trust. Armed with knowledge about what influences teachers' willingness to trust, they can work deliberately to establish the necessary positive conditions.

CREATING POSITIVE CONDITIONS FOR TRUST

- Foster connections
- Lighten the mood
- Clarify agreements
- Revisit the purpose or goal

People trust those with whom they perceive similarity. When I walk into a room, I can generally tell who is female and black, like myself, and if I know no one else, I might gravitate toward them. I cannot easily see who else just sent her son off to college for the first time, who recently traveled to China as I did, or who shares my passion for baking. To be sure, I'd be more likely to have a meaningful conversation with these connections than with a random person who matches my gender or race. Teacher/leaders can make a wide range of moves to help community members quickly see connections they share. These *connections* help to create positive conditions for trust. Teachers/leaders can

- Initiate one-on-one meetings with a check-in: keep it light and find a connection
- Start team meetings with icebreakers that help educators to identify passions and preferences they share
- Organize paired or small-group work by shared interests
- Encourage social events such as breakfasts, service projects, or happy hours

People are more inclined to trust when they are in a good mood. If a stranger offers you a high-five and you're in a good mood, you may be more inclined to say,

"Hey, why not?" and return the slap. If you are not, you're more inclined to stick to a "don't talk to strangers" rule and possibly pretend you didn't notice the stranger's outstretched hand. In fact, being in a good mood affects the way our brains function. It makes us more flexible and it enables us to deal with complexity (Nadler, Rabi, & Minda, 2010). It allows us to have a growth mindset and to feel hopeful about embracing new possibilities, instead of being fixed on the idea that the way things are is the way they always will be (Dweck, 2006). It makes sense, then, that a good *mood* would increase our willingness to make ourselves vulnerable. Teacher/leaders can

- Play fun music as colleagues enter for a team or staff meeting
- Use a colorful tablecloth to cover student desks during a team or staff meeting
- Arrange to rotate the role of bringing a healthy and fun snack to meetings
- Support or create a faculty Sunshine Club that can surprise faculty members on important days (work anniversaries) or less important days (National Banana Bread Day: February 23)
- Open a meeting by inviting colleagues to share stories of something a student did or said that made them laugh

People are more likely to trust if there is an agreement or contract in place. People's willingness to make themselves vulnerable is based on their belief that others will act appropriately. In our diverse school settings, there is a lot of room for ambiguity about what is "appropriate," and taking time to clarify *agreements*—through conversation or even in writing—can help. Teacher/leaders can

- Initiate a conversation about the school's core values, and name several to which we all are, or will agree to be, committed
- Take time to discuss and establish group norms, and create a routine for monitoring them
- Clarify roles and responsibilities of individuals as well as teams, and communicate these to all
- Create a proactive system for discussing when there might be an oversight, misunderstanding, or breach of the teachers' contract

People will be more prepared to trust if they believe in the cause. What are we working toward, anyway? Teacher/leaders who are able to communicate a vision that is clear and compelling will find that others want to share in it. If they have a transparent plan about how we'll reach that vision, one that allows stakeholders to believe it is possible and to see their necessary contribution to it, then community members will be willing to trust. Trust will require them to make themselves vulnerable, but it will feel like a worthwhile risk. The *goal* might be as large as a district improvement plan, or as small as a new grade-level plan for formative assessments. On any scale, teacher/leaders can

- Engage the community in sharing ownership of the plan: co-create it, critically review it, collaboratively revise it
- Communicate the vision and plan in multiple modes of representation: narrative, graphic, oral
- Share responsibility for monitoring the plan: create benchmarks, celebrate milestones, document successes, learn from challenges
- Support members to play an impactful role: match members to needs based on expertise, and ensure they have what they need to make authentic contributions
- Reference the vision and the key components of the plan routinely: show how everything we do ties back to it

With the right underlying conditions, community members will be favorably inclined to open themselves up to their colleagues and to the possibility of achieving the vision of their shared work. They might be more willing to trust. Our next charge is to strategically support teams and colleagues to strengthen all four types of trust.

Analyzing Existing Trust

Each of the four types of trust requires a different strategy to strengthen it. You wouldn't use a screwdriver to drive in a nail. If team members have not developed respect for each other, they will benefit from opportunities to recognize and connect about the values they share. If personal regard is lacking, connecting about shared values won't help. Members need opportunities to learn about each other's individual interests and concerns. When I see that a member doesn't follow through on a task, I may wonder whether the issue is competence (that is, the individual didn't know how). If so, perhaps I can teach that team member how to complete the task skillfully. Or is lack of integrity the problem (for example, if the team member doesn't feel committed to the responsibility)? In that case, perhaps some reflection on whether the team member volunteered or was "voluntold" can guide me in a conversation about the importance of fulfilling the responsibility and possible supports needed to do so. The strategy must match the problem.

The Team Trust Analysis Survey (see Figure 5.6) was designed to help educators determine what types of trust may be present or lacking so that they can be strategic in their approach to strengthening trust. In this tool, examples of low- and

FIGURE 5.6 TEAM TRUST ANALYSIS SURVEY

Leadership is influence and influence occurs through interaction. It's worth considering, then, what kinds of interactions are happening in your school, and what kinds of deliberate actions you might take to influence them in a positive way.

I. What kinds of interactions are happening?

Trust is an essential component of schools that are organized for student success. One reason trust is so complicated is that there are several different "types" of trust.

As you reflect on your school, determine the best response for each statement below. Consider the past 12 months as you answer.

Most teachers would say this is happening . . .

	throughout the school (4)	among several teams in the school (3)	by some individuals (2)	by few, if any (1)
1. Educators frequently compromise and agree with each other.	○	○	○	○
2. Educators acknowledge or celebrate each other's professional strengths and accomplishments.	○	○	○	○
3. Educators bad-mouth each other's teaching.	○	○	○	○
4. Educators co-develop better lessons together than they could have developed on their own.	○	○	○	○
5. Educators disagree productively.	○	○	○	○
6. Educators extend gestures of welcome and assistance to novice teachers.	○	○	○	○
7. Educators plan events, assemblies, and outings together.	○	○	○	○
8. Educators collaborate in setting goals, developing action plans, and carrying them out.	○	○	○	○
9. Educators seek assistance from colleagues when faced with knowledge gaps, challenges, or fears in their role.	○	○	○	○
10. Educators offer each other unsolicited assistance, advice, or feedback to help each other improve.	○	○	○	○
11. Educators divide up shared tasks to make the load lighter.	○	○	○	○

FIGURE 5.6 TEAM TRUST ANALYSIS SURVEY continued

	throughout the school (4)	among several teams in the school (3)	by some individuals (2)	by few, if any (1)
12. Educators share and use professional resources developed by each other.	O	O	O	O
13. Educators violate agreed-upon norms and core values.	O	O	O	O
14. Educators point out and celebrate shared accomplishments.	O	O	O	O
15. Educators collaborate to establish school-wide systems that everyone follows.	O	O	O	O
16. Educators disregard each other's needs.	O	O	O	O
17. Educators reach out in support when a colleague is having a bad day.	O	O	O	O
18. Educators refuse to work together.	O	O	O	O
19. Teachers feel they can share ideas and insights for improving the school with school administrators.	O	O	O	O
20. Educators reach out to exchange information about students they share.	O	O	O	O

II. Open Response

1. Respect: Can you describe any additional ways in which you and your colleagues show that you hear and value each other and demonstrate confidence that you will be heard and valued by each other?

2. Personal Regard: Can you describe any additional ways in which you and your colleagues take actions that extend beyond role obligations and have each other's individual interests at heart?

3. Competence: Can you describe any additional ways in which you and your colleagues demonstrate knowledge and respect of one another's professional expertise?

4. Integrity: Can you describe any additional ways in which you and your colleagues demonstrate confidence in one another's ability to follow through?

(continued)

FIGURE 5.6 TEAM TRUST ANALYSIS SURVEY continued

III. SCORE

Directions	Respect		Personal Regard		Competence		Integrity	
For the survey question numbers that appear at right, indicate your score (4, 3, 2, or 1) for that question in the box provided.	1		6		2		7	
	5		10		4		8	
	14		17		9		11	
	19		20		12		15	
Add your scores to obtain your subtotal for this type of trust								
ADD one point for each additional inter-action you described	+		+		+		+	
SUBTRACT your score for each of these red flags	18	–	16	–	3	–	13	–
Total								

IV. Post-Survey Reflection: What are your opportunities for influence?

1. **Review the score totals in the grid above:** What kinds of trust does this suggest may be prevalent, developing, absent, or threatened? Use your knowledge of the school to consider which underlying conditions may be support-ing or limiting trust.

2. **Review the range of scores in the grid:** Circle all of the 4s. Which kinds of trust are schoolwide, and which kinds of trust exist only in certain teams? Use your knowledge of those teams to consider what they have in common.

3. **Review any 1s in your survey:** Pick one or two and reflect upon the root causes. What stands in the way? What would have to happen before this example would be seen more widely in your team or school?

4. **Consider next steps for progress:** Describe one or two actions YOU can take. What resources, people, or training might you need?

high-risk interactions are scrambled in a questionnaire that invites educators to rate their perceptions of the extent to which each type of interaction is happening throughout the school. Since the list includes four positive examples and one negative example of each type of trust, results indicate the relative presence of each type of trust and alert users to common red flags.

The survey can be administered to individuals, teams, or whole faculty groups. Take the survey yourself to think about how it could be adopted or adapted to be most useful in your context. Here are a few notes to consider as you explore the survey:

- A Google Docs version of the survey, with calculations built in to the response spreadsheet, is available online. This will allow you to adapt the survey as needed (e.g., changing the focus from school to team), to easily manage survey responses, and even to leverage formulas to auto-calculate the scores.
- The sample interactions in the survey were compiled from those commonly reported by school teams. They do not represent the only ways or the most important ways each type of trust can be observed, as the survey has not been validated through research. The survey is meant to give direction to team members' conversations about trust and to stimulate team members' thinking about what the four types of trust look like in their own context.
- Consider using the survey to monitor the development of trust. Administer it at the beginning, middle, and end of the year.

Whether you reflect individually on the types of trust in your school or engage colleagues in doing so together, you will no doubt see opportunities to strengthen trust.

Taking Strategic Steps to Strengthen Trust

Recall that people need positive experiences with low-risk interactions before they can engage authentically in the kinds of high-risk interactions that are most important to school improvement. This principle guides our strategy for strengthening trust and our understanding of what it takes for leaders to stay in sync. After educators have had positive experiences taking small risks to acknowledge shared values or positive experiences, recognize common needs and preferences, share expertise, and cooperate to carry out low-stakes tasks, they may be willing to take bigger risks to acknowledge concerns that offer opportunities for growth, leverage needs and preferences to enrich the school, count on each other's expertise as an asset to grow everyone's practice and knowledge, and collaborate on decisions with higher stakes and bigger payoffs. Trust is not just a pleasant characteristic of the community, but instead is an asset that builds on respect to foster collaboration, on personal regard to capitalize on a variety of staff strengths, on competence to accelerate collective capacity, and on integrity to honor teacher expertise and push the team toward excellence.

The sections that follow examine how low-risk interactions inform our decisions to engage in higher-risk interactions and describe how teacher/leaders, both formally and informally, can create opportunities for community members to make positive discernments about respect, personal regard, competence, and integrity.

Respect. We respect each other when we recognize what makes all of us the same—our humanity. You have passions; I have passions. You have fears; I do too. We don't have to have the same passions and fears to respect each other; we simply have to acknowledge our differences as each other's truth and, therefore, as having value. This is important because to improve, schools need everyone's truth. The stakes are high for sharing a concern or disagreeing with others. One might be seen as a naysayer, a complainer, or a mean-spirited jerk. If community members do not feel their concerns will be respected and valued, they will not share them, and the school will lose a critical opportunity for growth.

We are more likely to risk sharing observations that raise concerns if we have first had positive experiences sharing observations that celebrate accomplishments. In fact, each positive observation we share helps contribute to a collective recognition of our school's strengths, what we value, and the things that make us proud. Grounded by a shared understanding of what we appreciate about our school, we are more likely to believe that others will want to hear our concerns, which represent potential threats to the very school we all appreciate.

This idea has practical implications for teacher/leaders who co-perform leadership in both formal and informal ways. Members in a school community may eventually learn about one another's passions, fears, and truths, and build a shared recognition of shared values. Why not give this process a boost? Figure 5.7 suggests what teacher/leaders can do to expand opportunities for community members to make positive discernments about respect.

Personal regard. We have personal regard for one another when we recognize the individual variation in our humanity. In many ways we are all the same, but we each want to be appreciated for our uniqueness, too. Our diversity of views and experiences is what makes our community strong, beautiful, and fun. If we each contribute only the assets that we have in common, we'll have an abundance of basic resources but nothing that inspires us to move beyond to something greater. We'll languish based on the lowest common denominator across our skill sets. But what does it take to get individuals to go beyond? It cannot be mandated, because everyone has something different to contribute. That should be seen not as a problem, but as an opportunity.

FIGURE 5.7 EXPANDING OPPORTUNITIES FOR POSITIVE DISCERNMENTS ABOUT RESPECT

Recognizing what makes all of us the same		
	Informal Teachers/Leaders	**Teachers/Leaders in Formal Roles**
Low Risk After educators have had positive experiences taking small risks that acknowledge shared values or positive experiences . . .	• Be a connector: help colleagues to discover commonalities they share • Reflect with others about the school's strengths and what they say about us as a community • Start a Twitter hashtag featuring #whatIloveabout [this school]	• Build time into meeting routines for colleagues to share good news from their classrooms/roles • Start meetings with a quick opportunity to connect and learn something new about each other (e.g., Why did you enter teaching? Tell about your favorite teacher.); look for common themes • Designate a bulletin board on which community members can post appreciations of one another and the school
High Risk . . . they may be willing to take larger risks to acknowledge concerns that offer important opportunities for growth	• Discuss your ideas for improvement with the team or the individual responsible • Support a colleague to turn complaints into improvement actions • Invite a colleague to work with you on a shared concern	• Establish an easy process for others to submit feedback or raise concerns: office hours, exit tickets, online polls, 3-2-1, and so on • Designate and protect time to critically reflect on events we have created together • Invite teachers to meet with you one-on-one to discuss what's going well and what they'd like to see improve

Individuals are more likely to extend themselves beyond basic role expectations when they have positive experiences with having done so in low-stakes situations. To be sure, there are those who hide their talents for fear of being pressed into service and then being left holding the bag. This is why fostering repeated experiences in which individual needs, passions, and preferences are recognized and celebrated—without any high-stakes consequences—is an important first step. As members build appreciation for others' individual talents, they build hope about what could be possible with all this talent, and they strengthen confidence in the capacity of everyone to contribute. They will be more likely to make themselves vulnerable and go beyond role expectations with confidence that others will act appropriately and do the same.

Too often, educators get to know only those with whom they work directly on their team or in their hallway. Figure 5.8 suggests deliberate steps teachers/leaders can take to foster personal regard.

Competence. We trust colleagues' competence in core role responsibilities when we have confidence in their expertise. Trusting in the competence of

FIGURE 5.8 EXPANDING OPPORTUNITIES FOR POSITIVE DISCERNMENTS ABOUT PERSONAL REGARD

Recognizing individual variation		
	Informal Teachers/Leaders	**Teachers/Leaders in Formal Roles**
Low Risk After educators have had positive experiences taking small risks to recognize individuals' needs, passions, and preferences . . .	• Arrange social events (e.g., happy hour, monthly breakfast or potluck lunch) to learn about each other's likes and dislikes, joys and sorrows • Ask about and honor colleagues' special needs: dietary, physical restrictions, allergies, and the like • Ask about and celebrate colleagues' special talents: language ability, carrying a tune, green thumb, and so on • Get to know novice teachers and those who are new to the school; help the community to see the unique contributions they bring to the community	• Celebrate work anniversaries with an opportunity to name and celebrate what we appreciate about the honoree(s) • Lead team members in discovering one another's work styles; discuss how we contrast and complement each other • Share your personal story: who you are and key influences shaping what you believe today; invite others to do the same
High Risk . . . they may be willing to extend themselves in ways that leverage individuals' needs, passions, and preferences	• Show your personal regard for others by committing acts that demonstrate you recognize their individuality (e.g., recommend a book, write a note) • Be an advocate for yourself, communicating what you need to thrive and your limits • Be an advocate for your colleagues	• Be transparent about how your personal passions and concerns shape and motivate you • Publicly acknowledge and celebrate ways in which educators' passions and preferences energize their work • Show recognition and gratitude when others choose to go beyond role expectations

colleagues is essential for moving beyond the traditional egg-crate structure of schools, in which the environment is designed to keep each teacher from coming into contact with the others, and instead fosters collaboration that enables schools to perform at higher levels (Quintero, 2017). Teachers want to give their students the best learning experience possible. In the calculus of whether they are better off working alone or with colleagues, teachers consider their estimation of colleagues' competence. Although underlying conditions, such as reputation or our knowledge of the credentials others hold, may influence our willingness to believe in others' competence, we generally build confidence in others' competence by seeing them in action.

Many people can talk the talk. We need to know who can get the job done and do it well. Once we have had a series of low-stakes opportunities to see what others are capable of, we will be more willing to invest in collaborative projects and to make ourselves vulnerable with confidence that these colleagues will act appropriately.

Most schools do not support colleagues to learn who is good at what throughout their organizations. This is a special problem in turnaround schools, in which the principal and half of the staff may be new. We need to be able to learn—quickly—about each other's areas of strength so that we can maximize our opportunities to learn from each other. Teacher/leaders can play a strategic role, as illustrated in Figure 5.9.

Integrity. We have confidence in colleagues' integrity when we believe they are committed to doing the right thing and meeting role expectations. Integrity is especially important in education because, as in all true professions, we deal with an urgent matter that we approach with a service ethic (Johnson, 2005). We espouse values about justice, hope, and opportunity, and we are expected to act in accordance with them. These values not only motivate each of us to be our best selves, but they also give us a sense of solidarity with other members of the profession. Most of us love to be challenged in a climate of mutual support and accountability for excellence, but this works only if we are all in. Are we all in? If I count on my colleagues, what is the risk that I will be let down?

FIGURE 5.9 EXPANDING OPPORTUNITIES FOR POSITIVE DISCERNMENTS ABOUT COMPETENCE

Recognizing colleagues' expertise		
	Informal Teachers/Leaders	**Teachers/Leaders in formal roles**
Low Risk After educators have had positive experiences taking small risks to identify, celebrate, and share expertise . . .	• Keep an eye out for teachers' strengths and acknowledge them—publicly and privately • Ask colleagues to share resources related to the strengths you've noticed • Share stories about what you have learned from your colleagues	• Solicit "shout outs" during a meeting: observations of each other's professional strengths • Invite colleagues who have attended a workshop to share their key takeaways • Organize a classroom walk-though rotation so that all can participate; focus on collecting positive examples of our priorities at work
High Risk . . . they may be willing to extend themselves to count on colleagues' expertise as an asset	• Invite a colleague to co-plan a lesson or unit with you • Solicit a colleague to give you feedback on a unit plan • Invite a colleague with requisite expertise to observe you and give you feedback on a particular strategy	• Schedule inquiry cycles focused on instructional rounds, looking at student work, implementing student interventions, pursuing National Board certification, and so on • Support vertical content teams to create or revise curriculum maps or to develop common formative assessments • Empower teachers to lead professional learning experience for their colleagues

We are more likely to trust in others' integrity when we have first had low-risk opportunities to see evidence that others' actions are in line with the values they espouse and those that we share as members of a profession. Most of us have had experiences with a colleague who says one thing and does another or agrees to collaborate and then deserts the project. So, the burden of proof is on others. Further, many of the contributions teachers make fly under the radar; we can't make positive discernments about them unless we know about them. The more opportunities educators have to see their colleagues' commitment at work, the quicker trust will be established.

Figure 5.10 presents examples of the many things that teachers/leaders can do to facilitate positive discernments and trust-building related to integrity.

Other Considerations in Strengthening Trust

Trust is required for effective shared leadership, and effective leaders share responsibility for cultivating trust. Teacher/leaders can take numerous steps to create opportunities for making positive discernments about their colleagues' respect, personal regard, competence, and integrity, and thereby to strengthen trust (see Figures 5.7 to 5.10). But each of these steps also creates an opportunity for making

FIGURE 5.10 EXPANDING OPPORTUNITIES FOR POSITIVE DISCERNMENTS ABOUT INTEGRITY

Recognizing colleagues' commitment to do the right thing and meet role expectations		
	Informal Teachers/Leaders	**Teachers/Leaders in Formal Roles**
Low Risk After educators have had positive experiences taking small risks to cooperate on carrying out tasks with low stakes and/or accountability . . .	• Invite collaboration: tap a colleague to join you in planning a field trip, cross-grade activity, or project • Share, "shout out," or otherwise publicly appreciate the contributions of others to collaborative work • Suggest ways in which teams can divide up shared tasks to make the work lighter	• Create opportunities for teachers to work together on "quick wins" such as planning school events: assemblies, parent engagement, field day, and so on • Encourage teams to identify and rotate meeting roles • Designate time to track tasks as they are assigned in meetings, and to recognize task completion in the next meeting
High Risk . . . they may be willing to collaborate on making decisions that have high stakes and/or accountability and stand to improve conditions for teaching and learning	• Invite collaboration: tap a colleague to join you in advocating for student services, instructional materials, or new resources • Convene a book study group around a teaching or learning priority • Find partners to join you in applying for a grant for a new resource or program that will meet your students' needs	• Recruit colleagues for a significant school improvement project with an action plan • Convene collaborators to create or revise a significant school policy through research, data collection, and policy monitoring • Assign teachers to formal leadership roles with clear expectations

negative discernments. For instance, you might open the door for candid feedback and find some teachers respond with ungrounded complaints or without tact. You might help teachers open up about their personal passions and preferences, only to find colleagues blatantly disagreeing with those preferences or simply showing they don't care. Once you open the door for teachers to share their areas of expertise, there are likely to be some colleagues who disagree with teachers' estimations of their own competence, and others may bristle against this violation of traditional egalitarian norms. And, if each week when a team reviews its task list, it finds that no one has completed the tasks, we'd be reinforcing the norm that no one need to do them.

By starting from the ground up and establishing a strong foundation of positive conditions, connections are formed and relationships are built that foster mutual accountability and increase the pressure to meet others' high expectations. Once colleagues begin to depend on each other, they won't want to let each other down.

Thinking about commitments of trust from beyond the faculty can be helpful too. When we're reminded of the trust that parents (who send us their babies), students (whose attendance is compulsory), and society (which relies on our success) have in us as educators, we are called to a higher, moral purpose to engage.

Once educators who have respect and personal regard for each other begin to believe their colleagues can be trusted to follow through on commitments and perform them well, they themselves are more likely to reciprocate: to take on commitments and strive to perform them well. In time, trust will increase educators' willingness to put themselves out there for the greater good of the school and to reach together for shared aspirations of student success.

A RETURN TO LARSON HIGH SCHOOL

The newly arrived coach at Larson High School recognized that this tight-knit faculty had a significant foundation of respect and personal regard for one another, but they did not yet have confidence in each other's core role competence or integrity (see the box "Four Types of Trust"). In fact, it seemed as though the respect and personal regard teachers had for one another was getting in the way: Teachers felt they were doing their colleague a favor by going along with her suggestion to create the parent communication log, even though most did not intend to use it. In addition, she recognized that they had not yet built respect or personal regard for her, as their new coach, a position they did not ask for or understand. The faculty would need to deepen their trust with each other and with the coach in order to enter into the kind of higher-risk interactions that would be important for reversing the downward trend in student achievement (see Figure 5.5). From what the coach had seen, the expertise needed to reverse that trend was in the building, but teachers were not yet willing to make themselves vulnerable enough to share it.

For the majority of the faculty, positive conditions were in place (see the box "Creating Positive Conditions for Trust"), but teachers' existing connections almost made it harder to establish new ones. There were no "getting to know you" activities built into the school year's launch, and there was little patience for icebreakers among this familiar crowd. If the coach were not new to the community, she would have introduced the faculty to the types of trust and how trust is built (see Figures 5.3 and 5.4), then had them complete the Team Trust Analysis Survey (see Figure 5.6) to help them recognize where they were stuck. But, not having established relationships of trust herself yet, she decided she would start by doing instead of explaining. She would start her own meetings with connecting activities that would allow her to get to know teachers while supporting them to deepen relationships with each other (see Figures 5.7 and 5.8). In addition, she worked with the principal to clarify and communicate the purpose of her role, so that there would be less ambiguity about what the expectations and limitations of her authority would be.

Meanwhile, as faculty trust grew beyond the personal to the professional domain in low-risk ways, the coach collaborated with the principal and other members of the leadership team to create opportunities for teachers to engage in higher-risk interactions and make positive discernments about each other's competence and integrity (see Figure 5.9 and 5.10). They supported teachers to attend professional conferences in teams, experiment together with newly learned ideas, and collaborate in presenting their learning to others working on similar goals. They provided release time for teachers to engage in vertical curriculum mapping retreats or collaborative unit planning. And, when supporting teachers with their professional goals, they referred teachers to colleagues with relevant strengths and offered release time for peer observation. Each of these occasions presented opportunities for teachers to see inside each other's practice, to see the value of their colleagues as professional resources, and to have confidence in one another's commitment to stronger professional practice. As a result, they began to initiate their own informal professional interactions, elevate the conversation in team meetings, and become more invested in opportunities to influence schoolwide conditions that support their instructional improvement.

Reflection

1. Review your responses to the context questions at the beginning of this chapter. What new reflections do you have, and what possibilities for action do you see?
2. How might the ideas and strategies from this chapter help teacher/leaders in your school to co-perform leadership more skillfully?

Learning to Lead Together

It's exciting to think about what could be accomplished in a school that truly maximizes its leadership capacity. Once we open our minds to the idea of tapping the leadership potential of every educator, we can imagine limitless capacity for improved teaching and learning, increased teacher/leader satisfaction and retention, and greater student success. Truthfully, though, these are only possibilities. More often than not, when everyone is leading, no one is following, and mayhem ensues. We are all familiar with the "too many cooks" syndrome, but in today's schools, we can't afford to have anyone leave the kitchen.

As this book illustrates, maximizing the leadership influence of all educators requires that leaders take care to get in sync. It requires leaders to have a shared vision, coordination across teams and within them, and strong relational trust. This is not something that will happen without deliberate effort. It requires commitment to learning to lead together.

Learning Together

It is easy to become overwhelmed by the many different and important demands on schools and the tremendous variety of skills educators have to be good at to meet those demands. We're overwhelmed when we each envision addressing all of these demands ourselves. Once we recognize that leadership is already distributed—that everyone within the school is already influencing one another's practice in direct and indirect, intentional and unintentional, positive and negative ways—it allows us to consider what conditions would be required and what educators would have to learn to deliberately influence and support each other in more direct, intentional, and positive ways, and in ways that leverage each educator's strengths.

Leadership is about setting direction and leading others in that direction. In a deliberately distributed leadership system, shared vision is paramount to ensuring all are leading in the same direction. Leaders at all levels, therefore, must learn to build consensus around a common goal and shared understandings of the plan to meet it. In fact, teacher/leaders need to practice this skill at all levels of leadership: What is the vision of this curricular change? This team? This mentoring relationship? Once we have a clear, shared vision of where we are heading, then we are each more likely to offer our own unique skills and experiences to the task of getting there, and the school can leverage a far greater range of the faculty's expertise than if one leader had merely pursued the goal solo or delegated the tasks to members who are not in tune with the "why" behind the work.

With all hands on deck and a destination for this boat, who should do what? If we're going to co-perform leadership effectively, everyone should be playing a role that matches their expertise. Too often in schools we don't know who is good at what, so we don't know what skills and experiences might be tapped for greater impact throughout the school. Teacher/leaders can work together to identify the range of expertise they and their colleagues may need to address the school's most pressing priorities, and together they can practice a repertoire of strategies for identifying and cultivating colleagues who have these skills.

Working in this new way represents a big change from the status quo. We're calling for teachers and other leaders to exert themselves in more frequent and more productive interactions with colleagues. We're thinking about teacher leadership as a culture change that involves all, not merely an initiative that includes a few. Leaders must learn to be attentive to the conditions that can support or limit these efforts and ensure these new ways of interacting can thrive. Communication is important within and across teams and roles. As the school learns and improves, communication routines will help all to learn from each other, grow with each other, and stay in sync.

The changes recommended here are not small. They ask both teachers and administrators to make themselves vulnerable while believing that their colleagues will act appropriately. They require these educators to have trust, yet a climate of trust does not happen by chance. Leaders must learn about the deliberate steps they can take to accelerate the development of trust and to sustain trust at the level needed to make risky changes in how we work together and communicate. Understanding the potential of what can be accomplished (as described in Chapters 1–4) can animate the commitment needed to take on the hard work of building trust. In fact, after reading this book, some teams will elect to start their work with Chapter 5's tools and strategies for establishing a strong foundation of trust.

Leading Together

What does it look like when educators are truly leading together? Following are vignettes from schools in which teacher/leaders have committed to learning to lead together, and they have done so using the resources in this book. Each vignette illustrates a different path and offers a model that may expand your thinking about how these resources can be modified to address specific improvement challenges and school contexts.

ACCELERATING SCHOOL TURNAROUND: HENRY GREW ELEMENTARY SCHOOL, BOSTON, MASSACHUSETTS

Henry Grew Elementary School (the Grew) is an urban elementary school serving approximately 260 prekindergarten through 5th grade students. After several years of extremely low performance and very little evidence of growth, in 2014 the school found itself in the first percentile relative to elementary schools statewide. In that year, the Massachusetts Department of Elementary and Secondary Education included the Grew on its short list of schools receiving "turnaround" status. As required by this designation, a stakeholder group would be convened to set the direction for an improvement plan, the principal and at least half of the staff would be replaced, and the state would provide support and accountability to ensure the school was on the move. The school would have three years to demonstrate significant improvement and close the performance gap between Grew students and their peers.

The stakeholder group, including parents, teachers, district leaders, and community partners, collaborated to create a vision for the school. Among their recommendations was the charge to "create teacher leaders." When Christine Connolly, a former district leader and instructional coach, was selected as the new principal, she took this charge to a new level and announced that all teachers would be teacher leaders at the new Grew. Her decision was based on a belief in teachers, but also influenced by a practical concern: Financial support from the state department of education would not last forever. Investments needed to both boost improvement efforts and ensure sustainability. An investment in special teacher leader programs or teacher leader positions would have left the school with the challenge of continuing those supports after the grant funds ended. Instead, Christy allocated a portion of these funds to ensure all of the school's leaders would have leadership coaching. Joining the team as leadership coach, I used many of the tools in this book to guide the Grew in learning to lead in sync. It was an investment in educators' relationships and capacities with promise for lasting impact long after supplemental funds dried up.

Christy and I engaged in frequent conversations about what should be "fixed" and what could be "flexible" in regard to teachers' leadership authority as individuals and as members of teams (see Figure 4.2). She articulated four fixed core values: **g**rowth mindset, **r**igorous teaching and learning, **e**quity and engagement, and **w**e are all leaders—GREW. She then recruited teachers committed to these core values and who were prepared to think flexibly and creatively together about how these core values should inform the new school's development. Teachers with diverse talents, passions, and experiences were drawn to this challenge. Due to the school's turnaround status Christy had hiring authority, and the Assets Inventory (see Figure 3.4) was useful for strategically staffing the school with the expertise needed for the task ahead. With teachers on board who were individually and collectively ready for this work, Christy outlined four schoolwide teams and worked with teachers to find the right place for each on one of those teams. One representative per grade level was on the Instructional Leadership Team. All other teachers, based on their skills and interests, were on the Family and Community Team, the Comprehensive Behavioral Health Model Team, or the Student Support Team.

The individuals and teams were in place, but they would have to learn to lead in sync. To give this the time and attention needed, each summer I led a four-day leadership retreat. Volunteers from each team were recruited and compensated with stipends. In the first year, Grew teacher/leaders thought about what it would take for the faculty to work together as skillfully as a crew team on our local Charles River (see the box in Chapter 1). We collaborated to unpack the turnaround plan and identify the work it required so that we could refine our teams' roles and purposes to meet those requirements and think about how they would do so in sync (see Figure 4.8). We thought together about types of trust required of that work (see Figures 5.2 and 5.3), and created routines to strategically build and maintain the trust needed to help faculty feel we could take those risks (see Figures 5.4 and 5.7–5.10; see also Berg, Connolly, Lee, & Fairley,

2018). In addition, teachers set individual leadership goals that would be the focus of yearlong coaching (see Figure 3.3).

In the second year, we examined our leadership alignment by mapping the co-performance of our teams (see Figure 3.2). We also worked on deepening our understanding of trust, our toolkit of strategies for strengthening it (see Figure 5.5), and our knowledge about how trust supports or limits our ability to give and receive feedback. In year three, we took a deeper look at our shared vision, compared it to our current reality, and pushed each other to think creatively about the gap between the two. We considered the implications for ourselves as individuals learning to co-perform leadership (see Figure 3.7) and for our school as a learning organization (see Figure 4.10). We also pushed ourselves to extend our deep understanding of trust to our relationships with students and families.

Between each summer leadership retreat, throughout the school year, the Grew crew meets in various team configurations, including bimonthly schoolwide team meetings and weekly grade-level team meetings. These teams engage in data inquiry routines that ensure we are monitoring progress at the individual, team, and school levels and making appropriate midcourse corrections to our plan. Members rotate through the facilitator role in these meetings, and each meeting ends with the team defining the agenda for the next meeting (see Figure 4.9). In this way, meetings are focused on the authentic problems and targets of instructional practice that teachers themselves have helped to identify as critical to their success with students.

Speaking of student success, the Grew has plenty of that too. The school has turned around on an accelerated pace. Whereas school performance started in the first percentile statewide, after the first year of turnaround status, Grew students had narrowed the gap with state averages and exceeded district averages in English language arts, math, and science. After the second year, the performance of Grew students exceeded the district once again in English language arts and science, and exceeded state averages for English language learners in English language arts and math. Importantly, the Grew has also met its goal of creating a culture of strong relationships and capacities among the staff. This is critical to sustaining improvement. The New Teacher Project's national Insight Survey has been useful for monitoring instructional culture. Although the national average for schools taking the survey in 2017 was 7.24, Grew Elementary School scored at the top of the index with a 10.0.

Many factors have contributed to the Grew's accelerated success. Paramount among them is the trust that has been deliberately cultivated and curated. Third grade teacher Emmanuel Fairley noted, "Our relational trust continues to develop every day in the small things we do for one another (like sharing paper at the copy machine or planning surprise baby showers) to the more formal, 'big' things we do, like sending out reminder e-mails for upcoming learning walks or helping brainstorm solutions to problems in our classrooms."

To be sure, this work is challenging. The investment teachers make in collaborative work on top of full-time teaching and in a context of high-stakes accountability is daunting and exhausting. Teacher leaders, including and especially the principal, work long hours and have difficult days. Yet, Emmanuel reflected, "The trust at school enables us to bounce back when things 'flop' or when times get tough, and I think that's important to reiterate; that while there is much success at the Grew, there are challenges that sometimes obscure the work. However, our relational trust, inside and outside of the classroom, is what sustains our success." The strong foundation of trust makes other important work possible—from working productively in teams, to tackling the hardest questions, to giving each other the feedback needed to continue on this productive path of learning to lead together.

ACTIVATING TEACHER LEADERSHIP: HAWTHORNE ELEMENTARY SCHOOL, LOUISVILLE, KENTUCKY

Hawthorne Elementary is an urban elementary school in Louisville, Kentucky. It is one of over two dozen schools that participated in the Activating Teacher Leadership Institute (ATLI) I led in 2015 and 2016 with my colleague John D'Auria to support Kentucky schools to re-envision how teachers and other leaders could be leading together in their schools. Hawthorne sent a team of teacher/leaders that included the principal and three classroom teachers to help the school identify, tap, and bolster the power of teacher leadership for increased student learning.

Although, in the aggregate, students' academic performance at Hawthorne is on par with state averages, the ATLI team from this school was concerned about the persistent performance gaps between certain student subgroups and their peers. These subgroups include African American, Hispanic, Native American, students with disabilities, students in poverty (qualified for free/reduced-price lunch), and English learners. In an effort to support schools to monitor this achievement gap, the state of Kentucky reports the scores of these groups as a composite subgroup called "non-duplicated gap group." The ATLI team wondered: Was the school maximizing teachers' expertise as a resource for addressing this problem? Sylvana Martin, the ATLI team facilitator, reflected, "We knew we had many knowledgeable people, but we were not able to tap into that because we didn't really know everyone's specific strengths."

The team recognized, too, that an effort to tap into teachers' expertise as leaders would require some preliminary work to support necessary cultural and structural shifts. Tools they acquired at ATLI guided their approach. They used the Teacher Leadership Conditions documents (see Figures 4.1 and 4.6) to assess their school's readiness for this work and to identify areas that would need attention. Sylvana recalled, "We learned that we needed to shape our culture to help teachers feel safe in being able to come to administrators to discuss concerns, and that we also needed to work on helping teachers stay positive and remind them that they are amazing at what they do." In response, greater attention was paid to the human side of the school's work. Sylvana recounted that the principal, Jessica Rosenthal, "took time during faculty meetings to help teachers take care of not only their physical health, but [their] emotional health as well."

Next, to identify teachers' strengths, the ATLI team prepared to complete the Assets Inventory (see Figure 3.4) by surveying teachers about their strengths. In doing so, they made two important adaptations. First, they thought together about which skill areas should be on the survey, taking care to include areas that were most critical for the identified learning gaps. Sylvana explained, "There are so many people who are masters at things that we need help with, and that can help us to make progress with our vision here at school. When we saw the Assets Inventory, we saw that it could break down into the areas that we need. Not just who can become more empowered and lead, but who can lead in the areas of our improvement focus. Now we know where to help teachers and who to go to for providing that help."

Second, they administered the inventory in two rounds. In the first round, teachers ranked the skills based on their confidence in those areas. In the second round, teachers identified areas in which they felt their peers had expertise. Sylvana explained how the results were used. "The coach and I met with each teacher individually. We shared with them what their peers shared about them and what they said about themselves. They would say, 'My peers think *this* about me?' It gave them extra confidence. 'If everyone has this much faith in me, I'm going to try it.' They saw how much they are valued by their peers." Jessica had a similar reflection. She said, "There were individuals who may not have been outspoken in the past, but who I recognized to be accomplished teachers. It was affirming for me to see that staff also recognized their expertise. And it was motivating to the teachers. It gave them a boost to get them to the table. We said, 'You're being invited because your colleagues recognize you have something to offer. You're someone they'd like to see as a leader.' As a result, it pulled them out of their classrooms to be bigger leaders in the school."

These two moves laid the groundwork for activating teacher leadership in a way that transformed the culture. "When our team members saw that teachers were good at one thing or another," Sylvana noted, "we dove into that area and pursued them." The ATLI team tapped those strengths by encouraging teachers to engage in peer observations with teachers who had been identified as having strengths in the specific areas of growth they wanted to work on. "We go and observe our partners or another grade level to offer ideas and models. The Assets Inventory helped us get this up and running."

As observations progressed, teachers came out of their shells. "Some people who had been overlooked, or were just shy, are actually now leading trainings," Sylvana said. For example, one staff member whom many colleagues identified as having strong classroom management has stepped into a new role of training staff members, mentoring novice teachers, and leading activities for the whole faculty. Sylvana reflected, "It's a new side of her, to see her shine! But at the same time, it is helping the school with stronger classroom behavior." Others, too, who were previously fearful of presenting before colleagues found the survey results to be the push they needed to share their expertise.

In fact, with the renewed faculty interest in leadership and a keener sense of the specific strengths teachers had to offer, Jessica explained, "Our instructional leadership team was able to take on a new life. New leaders who were not engaged in the past were able to move forward and share ownership of the leadership team." Composed of representatives from each grade level, this team became a place for teacher/leaders to make decisions together for the school. The ATLI team used the tools for designing teams and roles (see Figures 4.2 and 4.3) to describe the team's scope, clarify expectations, and recruit the right combination of people for the work required. Sylvana reflected, "Now we have an instructional leadership team that is solid. It's everyone, not just the principal, making decisions for the school. That's a huge change."

It is exciting that teachers were enthusiastic and engaged in these new ways, but the ultimate goal of this work was to increase the math achievement of a particular subgroup. State math assessments for the target population showed an initial increase after one year, with a return to previous levels in year two. Jessica explained, "We know math was a focus area, but we didn't know how to turn this leadership learning into results down to the level of the kids. We still struggle with this." But they struggle with it together. The ATLI team of teacher/leaders redoubled their efforts and attended a training together that could help them to identify individual students for targeted intervention and progress monitoring. As principal, Jessica reflected, "Because of some of the things we learned at ATLI, I pushed myself from the table and let the teachers reflect on what was being presented about Tier 2 and 3 instruction. Then I let them present that to the faculty. That helped move us into a totally different direction. If I had brought that to the table, I'm not sure we would have seen the same results, or that the faculty would have embraced it in such a collaborative way." Teachers led the way in designing a plan for interventions that are being offered in classrooms and as enrichment at the end of each day. Jessica reflected, "Now we really have seen a change in students because of these tiered supports. Teachers are learning how to utilize interventions, and we're seeing the progress with our students." The team now looks forward to seeing the next set of annual test results. It will be a treat to look at them together.

INCREASING SHARED OWNERSHIP OF IMPROVEMENT: DONALD MCKAY K-8 SCHOOL, BOSTON, MASSACHUSETTS

Donald McKay K–8 School is a urban elementary school serving approximately 800 students. When Jordan Weymer took over as principal in 2013, the school was ranked in the sixth percentile for performance relative to other Massachusetts schools of the same type. Jordan took swift and deliberate steps to set clear expectations and organized teachers into teams so that he and his administrative team could support teachers to meet these expectations. This approach was effective. Three years later, in 2016, the school was identified as a top-tier "Level 1" school and had moved into the 30th percentile for performance. Jordan was pleased but not yet satisfied. He set his sights on making this good school a great one. He said,

"We're Level 1, but we still have a ways to go." The key, in his view, would be to "switch from a hierarchical top-down vision to one being created by a group of teachers."

Jordan and I began working together to reflect on his goals for his staff. "I've seen teachers' powerful abilities to help their colleagues raise the level of their practice," he told me. "I want to leverage that. I'm obsessed with creating a learning culture here. How does a teacher leader guide their colleagues in powerful professional learning?" We used many of the ideas and tools in this book to turn this question back on teachers to answer.

We used the Team Design Tool (see Figure 4.2) to draft a plan for a new teacher leadership team (TLT) that would plan and support the improvement of student and teacher learning. This draft was used to recruit teachers representing each grade level and content team. We then brought this new team together for three full days in June to revisit the draft, strengthen it with their feedback, and flesh it out into a shared vision of the work we would do together.

During the retreat, teachers created team metaphor maps (see Figure 4.8) to illustrate how our team's work would interact and intersect with other teams in the school. We thought together about "improvement," recognizing that working together toward it would require a clear, shared understanding of the high-level teaching and learning we would be improving toward, a standard we dubbed "the McKay Way." We spent time understanding how trust is built (see Figures 5.2 and 5.3), and we practiced trust-building activities (see Figures 5.7 and 5.8), which not only helped teachers to develop confidence in strategies they could use with their own teams but also helped to strengthen trust within our new TLT. We discussed the roles team members would take in guiding their colleagues' professional learning and in tracking our progress toward achieving the McKay Way. We also discussed teachers' fears and hopes about their new roles, and teachers took a self-assessment survey of the skills they have (see Figure 3.4) and the leadership skills they need (see Figure 3.3) to help each identify personal leadership goals important to their success. Teachers were honest in discussing their fears, hopes, and learning needs. The challenge ahead would require a lot of work and would involve a significant amount of risk. Some teachers felt unsure if they could do it, but they were encouraged by the safe community we had created to take that risk together.

When teachers returned from the summer, they jumped right into the work. They volunteered to lead trust-building activities that launched the faculty's back-to-school meetings, and they dove right into their new roles as leaders of their professional learning communities (PLCs). In bimonthly TLT meetings, the team laid out a plan to engage all colleagues, families, and students in conversations about their expectations for teaching and learning (see Figures 2.2 and 2.3). They used the data from these conversations to articulate the kind of school McKay aims to be, and to establish the McKay Way. Jordan reflected, "The value of having teachers create the expectations, rather than 'receive' them from me, is tremendous." With authentic shared ownership of the target for improvement, TLT members collaboratively identified instructional priorities needed to meet the target, they led inquiry cycles to help colleagues learn and strengthen these practices, and they organized peer observation and feedback opportunities to help each other progress. Jordan recalled, "There is so much more teacher-directed work happening, where the focus used to be administrator determined. They are facilitating PLC meetings and making explicit connections to what we're doing in [the] TLT."

This new role was a real shift for these teachers and their colleagues. Thus, we invested time during our retreat and throughout the year in strengthening teacher/leaders' leadership skills, collectively and individually. We also reserved time in TLT meetings to reflect on our leadership and collaboratively troubleshoot facilitation dilemmas. Teacher leaders rotated meeting roles in the TLT meetings. When it was each teacher's turn to facilitate, I met with that teacher one-on-one to support them in planning an engaging agenda that would address the objectives (established by the team at the end of the last meeting) while also engaging colleagues' adult learning needs. In addition, I used my planning meetings with teachers to revisit each teacher's own personal leadership goals and provide individualized support in using the many technology-based tools (see Figures 4.9 and 4.10) that help us to communicate effectively and stay in sync.

"Empowerment of teachers has been huge," according to Jordan. Teachers agree. In a midyear check-in, teachers reported feeling more confident in creating their common planning time agendas, keeping those meetings on track, and even supporting their colleagues to lead. In reflection, Jordan identified the June retreat as critical to establishing shared ownership of the team's charge. "It gave teachers time to think about and personalize the role. We went off-site and away from the distractions of the school environment, and we honored their professionalism with a nice setting." This felt like a worthwhile investment to ensure the team members had time and space before the new school year began to develop a new vision of themselves as professionals.

In addition, Jordan felt that the themes explored in these three days—shared vision, co-performance, and trust—and addressing them together, with him as a participant learning alongside teachers, helped all to see each other differently. Jordan reflected with honesty about his own change, and ways in which the retreat helped him to feel ready for the change. "Learning alongside teachers was essential. It alleviated some of my fears and anxieties about taking on this work. I saw teachers doing amazing stuff, and it helped me to know that they are ready. It's a gamble to release responsibility after being the primary instructional leader for these four years. In working closely with them for that amount of time, it helped me to feel confident that they are ready for this."

The retreat also gave teachers a peek at what this change might mean for their relationships with each other, and helped to increase their willingness to take the leap. In this large K–8 school, teachers do not regularly develop professional relationships beyond their immediate colleagues. Working together to explore the ideas and activities (in this book) required them to collaborate as a team and get to know one another more deeply. One teacher reflected, "I feel more comfortable talking to people from outside of my grade span. Finding things we have in common has helped to build trust." As teachers came to know each other in a new way, their confidence in each other—and in their collective ability to take on their new charge—was built. At the end of the June retreat, one teacher noted, "I feel like we made some real progress in determining concrete goals and a purpose for the year. I feel confident, and having activities that are engaging and focused on building trust has been helpful." Teachers left the three retreat days with a clearer idea of the new work ahead. To be sure, they had fears about the unknowns, but they also were buoyed by the trusting new relationships they had built and that they were confident would help support them through challenges.

Jordan's role has shifted dramatically. He is no longer facilitating teacher's team meetings, as he was before the TLT was launched. He has gone from being the organizer to being a resource, supporting teachers with what they need to lead. This shift is not made without reservations, but it comes with great rewards. He says, "We've had great success with things being done from the top down. There will be concern when you shift the power. When you shift who is steering the ship, who is charting the course of the school, and it's not the captain anymore—it's the crew—you worry about getting off track. It's easier to stay on track with one person calling the shots and holding the map, but sometimes that is not the most impactful journey. So, letting teachers chart the course is important, even when there is some anxiety with it. They are growing in impactful ways, and my role is to support them. It's more time consuming, but when we're getting teachers, families, and students involved, it's a change for the better."

TRANSFORMING PROFESSIONAL LEARNING: BEECHWOOD ELEMENTARY SCHOOL, BEECHWOOD, KENTUCKY

Beechwood Elementary is a suburban elementary school outside Cincinnati, Ohio, in Fort Mitchell, Kentucky. The school, which serves approximately 725 students in kindergarten through 6th grade, is a National Title I Distinguished School, and the district routinely receives recognition from *Newsweek, US News & World Report,* and the Kentucky Department of Education for its academic ranking. When I began working with this team in June 2015 as part of the second cohort of the Activating Teacher Leadership Institute (ATLI) in Kentucky, teacher/leaders noted that although the percentage of Beechwood students achieving in the top two performance levels far exceeded the state averages, results varied by subject area, student subgroup, and classroom. After examining these data, the principal and four teachers put their heads together to think about how to maximize teachers' diverse areas of expertise throughout the school.

They did so with caution, for two reasons. First, the past year had already brought significant changes, including a new principal, and there was some resistance among the staff to trust in further change. The culture and climate would have to improve first. Second, they knew that teachers were not accustomed to talking about their professional strengths or turning to each other for expertise. They realized that teachers would need encouragement and support to recognize their individual skills as organizational assets.

The team resolved to start by introducing a fresh vision of shared responsibility for school improvement. The principal took a back seat while the teacher leaders used the crew video (see the box in Chapter 1) to inspire the faculty to consider the impact a more coordinated, collective effort could have on all students, and invited colleagues to complete the

Assets Inventory (see Figure 3.4) as a self-reported survey of the expertise and experience each had to contribute. They then celebrated these "super-powers" through a bulletin board in the teachers' room and invited teachers to use this wall as a resource so that, as one teacher explained, "If there is someone who is really strong in classroom management, you can use that person to help you." But would they? Teacher leader Ashley Ritchie reflected, "Teachers saw that the principal was behind us and trusted us, that he was letting teachers try something new and take the lead." Teachers responded positively and began turning to one another for support. "It was really neat to see people getting involved in that way."

In the following year, the work evolved and transformed the school's professional learning communities. Teachers identified the top areas in which they wanted to improve, and mini-PLCs were organized throughout the year by these topics. Every teacher was given a chance to chair a PLC in an area they felt confident about, and when not leading a session, teachers could choose which PLC to attend based on their needs. Ashley reflected, "It has been a real culture change. It has created an environment in which everyone feels safe, even to share things that aren't working, and to be vulnerable, even with people who you don't work with every day. People are no longer complaining about professional development. People are now saying, 'Yeah, I can lead a meeting. I can get involved.' It is not a competitive thing. It is helping people feel included—everyone has something to contribute to the school."

The impact on teachers' practices can be seen throughout the school. In the technology PLC, teachers led an introduction to parent communication tools and their colleagues were able to set them up before they left the session. Within a week, several teachers had also joined Twitter and were using other new tools in their classrooms. In another PLC, a teacher shared a strategy she has used for monitoring the impact of behavior interventions: placing a piece of tape on her pants to make it easy to track tally marks throughout the day. Small signs—from seeing a new colleague pop up on Twitter to catching a colleague with tape on her pants—provide palpable evidence of the transformation that is happening as teachers not only take the lead in professional learning but welcome the opportunity to follow each others' lead.

The impact on the school's culture and climate has also been quite apparent. In Kentucky, schools' professional climate and culture are routinely monitored via the TELL Kentucky survey, which solicits teachers' perceptions of "Teaching, Empowering, Leading, and Learning."

Beechwood's 2017 TELL data reveal a significant jump from 2015 levels, such that the school's culture and climate data are now above district and state averages on relevant indicators, including teachers being recognized as experts, trusted decision makers, and leaders; professional learning is aligned, is collaborative, and enhances student learning; and overall, school is a good place to work and learn. In fact, for the first year in recent memory, the school has not lost any teachers to attrition.

At Beechwood Elementary today, every teacher is a leader. That is, every teacher is empowered and supported to be a positive influence on the quality of colleagues' teaching. Although the school still has some formal teacher leader roles, many have become unnecessary and were eliminated. Ashley explained, "We've gotten away from those bigger roles. Those roles are not as important because everyone has the chance to be equally involved. Now, instead of identifying 'superheroes,' these days we're talking more about teams that include everyone." Her colleague Amanda Klare agreed: "Through our work with ATLI, I feel like we were able to help every teacher find the leader within. They were already leaders, but through the Assets Inventory, they were able to hone in on the leadership skills they had to offer the school. The best end product is this: Teachers and administration all being on the same team means that students win too."

Learning to Lead Together

This book advocates that teachers, principals, and other school leaders should commit to being more strategic about how they co-perform leadership in their schools. It provides ideas, tools, and strategies that support educators to develop the shared vision, coordination, and trust needed to accomplish this. As a final word, it is useful to review why this is work that must be pursued—and nurtured—together.

First, leadership co-performance requires shared understandings and language for leadership practice. The conversations teacher/leaders have as they negotiate this new way of working and communicating—for example, through pursuing the strategies in this book—allow them to have shared experiences that give their language shared meaning and will help keep the conversation going and growing. They cannot accomplish this if they pursue this learning separately.

Second, one of the benefits of leadership co-performance is that it allows each teacher/leader's skills and experiences to be an asset throughout the school. There is no one "right" way to do this, as each set of teacher/leaders is unique, balancing one another in their own ways, and in ways they need to discover for themselves over time. As teacher/leaders work together, they learn about each other's strengths and grow to complement each other's skills. As they do so, they create the kind of work environment in which all members of the community are valued, challenged, and inspired.

Third, individuals and organizations have a dynamic relationship. If individuals grow and learn but their organizations do not, those individuals are unable to maximize their new learning due to constraints of the old system. Similarly, when schools introduce changes, such as new roles or new work routines, and the individuals working within them do not also develop new learning, those individuals are unprepared to maximize the advantages that the organizational changes were meant to afford. By pursuing this work together, teachers and administrators are able to balance one another's investment and respond in ways that keep both individual and organizational learning on a path of improvement.

Finally, and most important, teachers, principals, and all school leaders must pursue this work together for students' sake. Our schools already contain much of the knowledge, skill, and experience needed to ensure all students can achieve. We get in the way of our own success when we fail to come together around a shared vision for what student success looks like and how we'll work together to meet it. We further stymie efforts when we overlook ways to tap into existing expertise in service of that vision, or we let our egos get in the way of establishing the trust that is needed to make necessary changes. We must commit to learning to lead together so that we can bring all available resources to bear on student learning. We must pursue this work together because students can't wait.

So, what are you waiting for? Grab your team and get started!

Appendix A

Annotated List of Figures and Blank Templates

The following table is designed to help you easily select and locate the examples, tools, activities, and templates from this book that you would like to use with colleagues to plan and co-perform leadership. Since several of the tools are provided in the text with sample data, blank copies are provided in this appendix for your use. In addition, you may download the planning tools* at **http://www.ascd.org/ASCD/pdf/books/berg2018.pdf.**

Figures	Information, Ideas, and Examples	Planning and Reflection Tools	Team Activities	Notes
Figure 1.1: Range of Teaching Knowledge and Skill Required Within a Typical High School	x			Teaching is complex work, requiring a vast array of knowledge and skills. It is not possible that one person can have mastered all of the expertise required in a school. Use this list to reflect on the distribution of expertise across your team or your faculty.
Figure 1.2: Leadership Tracking Tool*		x		Where is leadership already happening in your school? Use this organizer to help you identify the interactions (tasks, activities, routines, etc.) that influence student learning and the people who are involved.
Figure 1.3: How Teacher Leaders Influence Student Learning	x			In what ways are teachers influencing the quality of teaching beyond their own classrooms in your school? Teacher leaders can have an impact on student learning in three main ways.
Figure 1.4: Stakeholders and the Evidence They Have About the System	x			Each stakeholder in the system has access to different kinds of evidence about the system. Use this diagram to reflect on the opportunities and challenges the differences present for leadership co-performance.

Figures	Information, Ideas, and Examples	Planning and Reflection Tools	Team Activities	Notes
Figure 1.5: Points of Leverage for Improving the Quality of Teaching, by System Stakeholder	x			Why not just work alone? Use this diagram to stimulate thinking and discussion about the unique and important influence each stakeholder has in the system, and the interdependent nature of these influences.
Chapter 1 box: Crew Video Activity			x	Is your faculty or team leading in sync? Use this activity to support colleagues to develop a shared understanding of the importance of coordinating their efforts and having a shared commitment to doing so.
Figure 2.1: Forming Our Own Judgments About the Quality of Teaching	x			What information are we using to make judgements about quality? Use this checklist to identify your own priorities and assumptions and to stimulate conversation about them with colleagues.
Figure 2.2: Indicators of Quality Throughout the System*		x		Are you able to articulate your vision of quality teaching? Use this organizer, individually or with a team, to help you tease out the indicators of teaching quality from other indicators in the system.
Figure 2.3: Stimulating Conversations About the Quality of Teaching	x			How can you increase everyday opportunities to engage in conversations about quality teaching? Doing so helps establish a shared vision about it. Use these examples to reflect on where and how frequently such conversations are happening in your school.
Figure 2.4: Sync or Float			x	What does skillful co-performance around a shared vision feel like? Your team might not be able to rent a crew boat, but if you have a broomstick you can try this activity to experience and stimulate discussion about coordinated effort.
Figure 2.5: Diversity Rounds			x	Including all perspectives in the conversation about vision can be a challenge. Is it worth it? What is the value of diverse perspectives? Try this interactive activity with your team to stimulate reflection on that question.
Figure 2.6: Multiple Data Sources	x			Shared vision for what? Examining data together helps teams develop a shared understanding of who our students are and a common language for discussing their needs.
Figure 2.7: Indicators of Quality (Reprise)*		x		What do your students need from you? Use this organizer to revisit the work started in Figures 2.1 and 2.2 with your particular students in mind, and work toward consensus on what quality teaching is in your context.
Chapter 2 box: A Common, Shared Vision: Massachusetts	x			Perhaps you think your community is too large to include everyone in a conversation about shared vision. Reflect together with your team about this case, in which Massachusetts engaged stakeholders from throughout the state in just such a conversation.
Figure 3.1 Commitment to Personalized Learning (included for reference)	x			Image illustrating the black box between commitment and action.

Figures	Information, Ideas, and Examples	Planning and Reflection Tools	Team Activities	Notes
Figure 3.2: Co-performance Mapping*		x		Who needs to sync up with whom? Use this tool to reorganize the information you gathered in Figure 1.2 and to identify leaders who influence the same leadership functions. Pay attention to these leaders' co-performance of leadership.
Figure 3.3: Teacher Leadership Expertise Inventory	x			What do teacher leaders need to know and do? What do they need to learn? Use this inventory of teacher leader skills to identify the competencies and learning targets required for a particular role.
Figure 3.4: Assets Inventory*		x		Who is good at what among your faculty members? Too often we don't know one another's strengths, which limits our ability to tap them as assets. Use this tool to collect an inventory of expertise and staff teams strategically.
Figure 3.5: Professional Standards for Educational Leaders	x			What do all educational leaders need to know and do? Use these Professional Standards for Educational Leaders to reflect on your own leadership practice.
Figure 3.6: Teacher Leadership Frameworks	x			What do teacher leaders need to know and do? Compare and contrast these three national efforts to articulate the competencies of teacher leaders.
Figure 3.7: Teacher Leadership Skills Alignment with the Professional Standards for Educational Leaders	x			This table illustrates alignment of skills from the Teacher Leader Expertise Inventory (Figure 3.3) with the Professional Standards for Educational Leaders (Figure 3.5). Use it with your team to plan professional learning for teacher leaders and administrators together.
Figure 4.1: Conditions Conducive to a Culture of Teacher Leadership	x			Use the conditions and sample strategies in this table to reflect together with your team about whether you have maximized conditions conducive to a culture of teacher leadership.
Figure 4.2: Team Design Tool*		x		When creating a new team, what are the boundaries on the team's discretion? Use this tool to support collaboration between the principal and team members to shape the team's charge.
Figure 4.3: Role Design Tool*		x		Plan new teacher leader roles by starting with the end in mind: What are the intended outcomes for students? Use this tool to support logic modeling in the role design process.
Figure 4.4: Role Description Template*		x		Everyone benefits when the goals, expectations, supports, and accountability of formal teacher leader roles are laid out clearly. Use this template to create a teacher leader role description.
Figure 4.5: Fifty Teacher Leader Roles	x			How might teachers lead? Use this list of 50 teacher leader roles to expand your thinking about the ways in which teachers might be a positive, intentional influence on the quality of teaching beyond their own classrooms.

Figures	Information, Ideas, and Examples	Planning and Reflection Tools	Team Activities	Notes
Figure 4.6: Conditions Important for the Success of Formal Teacher Leadership	x			What do teacher leaders in formal roles need to succeed? Use the conditions and sample strategies provided here to ensure you have set up these teacher leaders for success. (See also Figure 4.1.)
Figure 4.7: Leadership Co-Performance Models and Leadership Models Cards			x	They say it takes two to tango. This exercise supports two leaders (or teams) to work out their dance steps.
Figure 4.8: Metaphor Maps			x	What is a given team's relationship with the school and/or with the other teams in the school? Use this activity to surface assumptions about how a team functions and interacts with other teams.
Figure 4.9: Annotated Meeting Agenda Template*		x		How can we share leadership of a meeting? A meeting agenda that is complete with everyone's role spelled out and a clear plan for addressing meeting objectives makes the facilitator's thinking visible, and makes it easier for others to effectively follow the facilitator's lead.
Figure 4.10: Shared Filing Cabinet	x			How can educators in our school build on each other's work and stop reinventing the wheel? Use these guidelines to create a shared electronic filing cabinet so that teachers can have real-time access to the information they need to do their work.
Figure 5.1: Engagement, Productivity, and Inspiration (included for reference)	x			Image illustrating what happens to engagement, productivity, and inspiration in a climate of trust.
Chapter 5 box: Four Types of Trust	x			Image illustrating key distinctions in the four types of trust.
Figures 5.2 and 5.3: Types of Trust Cards (plus Exploration)			x	What distinguishes the four types of trust? Use this card deck to compare and contrast them with your team using a jigsaw, teach-in, or text-rendering protocol.
Figure 5.4: Process Model for Building Trust in Schools	x			How is trust built within a community? Use this model to create a strategic approach to the development of trust.
Figure 5.5: Examples of Low- and High-Risk Interactions	x			What do low- and high-risk interactions look like? Use these examples to reflect on the kinds of risks teachers are taking in your school and to expand your thinking about the kinds of interactions you would like to cultivate.
Chapter 5 box: Creating Positive Conditions for Trust	x			List of four key ways to create positive conditions for trust.
Figure 5.6: Team Trust Analysis Survey			x	What types of trust do colleagues have for each other in your school? Use this survey to identify the types of interactions educators are having and reflect on opportunities to influence them.
Figures 5.7 to 5.10: Expanding Opportunities for Positive Discernments about Respect, Personal Regard, Competence, and Integrity	x			How do you create opportunities that support development of trust? Use the ideas in these tables to expand your thinking about the roles that informal and formal teacher/leaders can play in supporting the development of trust.

Leadership Tracking Tool

Use the provided organizer to help you identify the interactions (tasks, activities, routines, etc.) that influence student learning in your school and the people who are involved.

Leadership Functions Necessary for Learning[1]	Interactions What tasks, activities, or routines occur in your school to influence this? In what ways is this being modeled, monitored, or advanced through dialogue?	People Involved Who are the people or teams involved in these interactions, in both intentional and unintentional ways?
School Learning Climate In what ways do our school's aims, values, and culture provide a focus on teaching and learning for students, teachers, administrators, and the wider community?		
Professional Capacity What ways does our school have for building individual and organizational knowledge about effective teaching and learning?		
Shared Instructional Expectations In what ways do educators engage in dialogue that leads to shared expectations about teaching and learning and/or influences classroom practice?		

Leadership Tracking Tool continued

Leadership Functions Necessary for Learning[1]	**Interactions** What tasks, activities, or routines occur in your school to influence this? In what ways is this being modeled, monitored, or advanced through dialogue?	**People Involved** Who are the people or teams involved in these interactions, in both intentional and unintentional ways?
Family and Community Involvement In what ways does our school involve students, parents, and the wider community as partners in supporting student learning and their own learning?		
Student Outcomes In what ways are we accountable for the impact of instruction on learning?		
Other If we were to ask educators in our school to name the tasks, activities, and routines that have the most significant impact on the quality of the teaching and learning in their classrooms, what would they say? If they were not already captured above, add them here.		

Examine the third column. These are all leaders.
- What patterns do you notice? What's missing?
- What was predictable to you? What surprised you?
- What do you wonder?
- What kind of small, strategic moves could increase the positive impact that formal and informal leaders are having in your school?

[1]School leadership encompasses responsibility for many aspects of schooling, from school operations, to personnel management, to program implementation. The leadership functions in this tool, adapted from *Organizing Schools for Improvement* (Bryk, Sebring, Allensworth, Easton. & Luppescu, 2010) and the National Center for School Leadership's model of learning-centered leadership (Southworth, 2005), encompass only the leadership functions that are most directly concerned with the quality of teaching and learning.

Indicators of Quality Throughout the System

Considering your context and the perspective of your current role, *sort the indicators* from Figure 2.1 into the columns below: Which are conditions? Determinations? Outputs? Results? In the process, if additional indicators occur to you, be sure to add those, too.

Conditions "of the context"	Determinations "of the educators"	Outputs "of the students"	Results "of the system"
Long-Term Inputs	*Short-Term Inputs*	*Short-Term Outcomes*	*Long-Term Outcomes*

What is quality teaching?

Review your lists above and consider the following questions:

1. Are there any patterns? Any surprises? Where do your "top five" priorities fall?
2. What do you need to make strong decisions about each determination? What can/do you do to influence others to make stronger determinations?
3. How do your outputs relate to your determinations?
4. Take a critical look at the "Conditions" and "Determinations" columns: You placed indicators in the columns based on current policies and practices in your context. Are there any indicators you would move? That is, what do you believe *should* be up to teachers, individually and collectively?

Try using the indicators in the "Determinations" column to answer this question: What is quality teaching?

Indicators of Quality (Reprise)

What do our students need from us? (What factors will contribute to desired outcomes?) What is high-quality teaching?		What do our students need? (What results are important?) What is high-quality learning?	
Conditions	**Inputs**	**Outputs**	**Outcomes**
Long-Term Inputs	*Short-Term Inputs*	*Short-Term Outcomes*	*Long-Term Outcomes*

Consider these questions together with your colleagues or leadership team:

1. *Indicators of quality:* What are our assumptions about what each looks like at a high level? What are the implications for students if we have multiple (formal and informal) leaders with different assumptions?

2. *Knowledge of students:* How does our knowledge of students affect our determinations about the quality of these indicators? About priorities?

3. *Underlying values:* Ultimately, our assumptions derive from underlying values that we hold. Together, can we identify them?

4. *Work toward agreement:* What expectations can we agree upon? Add adjectives, quantities, and qualifiers before each indicator.

5. *Identify and agree upon priorities:* Which indicators are most important for these students? Which should we focus on first?

6. *Consider the nested system:* Schools are nested within districts, and districts within states. Schools inherit the priorities and mission statements of the systems in which they reside. What important part does our school play in the district's mission? How does our vision of quality teaching align with the district's mission?

Co-Performance Mapping

In the first column of the table below, list the key teacher/leader roles and teams that you have in your school (e.g., principal, instructional leadership team members, grade-level team members, literacy coach). (You may have identified them in Figure 1.2.) Note that every teacher is likely a member of some team and, as such, could be considered a teacher/leader.

For each teacher/leader role or team, use the remaining columns to list the tasks, activities, or routines with which they are involved related to each leadership function. Include indirect, informal, and unintentional influence on the quality of teaching and learning.

Leaders	Leadership Functions Necessary for Learning				
	School Learning Climate	Professional Capacity	Shared Instructional Expectations	Family and Community Involvement	Student Outcomes	Other

Co-Performance Mapping continued

Leaders	Leadership Functions Necessary for Learning					
	School Learning Climate	Professional Capacity	Shared Instructional Expectations	Family and Community Involvement	Student Outcomes	Other

When you're done:

1. Review each function (column) in your grid:

» Is each function addressed adequately? Are there gaps and redundancies?

» Are there tasks, activities, tools, systems, and routines in each column that provide opportunities for interaction throughout the year? Or only sporadically?

» Do these interactions have a strong or weak influence on the leadership function?

2. Observe the distribution of teacher/leaders' influence across the grid:

» How aware do you feel teacher/leaders are of the influence they exert within each function?

» To what extent are they aware of who else is influencing this function (intentionally or unintentionally)?

» Are routines in place to ensure communication and coordination among these leaders?

» What actions might be taken to influence the formal distribution of leadership around this leadership function? By whom?

» What actions might be taken to influence the informal distribution of leadership around this leadership function? By whom?

Source: Functions are adapted from Organizing Schools for Improvement (Bryk et al., 2010) and the National Center for School Leadership's model of learning-centered leadership (Southworth, 2005).

Note: You can also choose another framework or just identify a leadership function on your own. Be sure to pick one that identifies what has to be accomplished by leadership, not a list of tasks to be done. Another list of leadership functions is found in Copland & Knapp's (2006) *Pathways to Student, Professional and System Learning.* This is a much broader list of functions that includes many with an indirect influence on learning.

Assets Inventory, Part A: Expertise

List all members of the team or faculty in the first column.

Use the codes provided to indicate the strengths of each member. This can be based on member self-reports, peer reports of each other's strengths, or leadership team estimations. Then indicate any network affiliations or credentials members have that may indicate additional relevant expertise, experience, or opportunities to learn.

Names	Knowledge and Skills Codes: 2 = strength; 1 = demonstrated; 0 = don't know/no evidence												Networks and Credentials	
													Membership in Professional Associations or Networks	Special Skills, Certifications, and/or Training

Review the sample data provided above:

- What do you notice? What patterns do you see?
- To what extent do strengths align with student needs and school priorities in your context?
- How might teachers' strengths be utilized as assets throughout this school?
- How might teachers' expertise be cultivated strategically to meet local needs and priorities?

Assets Inventory, Part B: Formal Roles

After examining the data in Part A, copy the names in the first column of Part B. In addition, list all of the school's key teams in the Team Assignments row.

Then use the space and codes provided to indicate members' individual formal roles and team assignments.

Names	Individual Roles **Formal Roles** (e.g., literacy coach, lead teacher, department head, teacher-in-charge, mentor)	Team Assignments Codes: 2 = team facilitator; 1 = member; 0 = inactive/nonparticipating member									

Review your inventory:

- What do you notice? What patterns do you see in who is holding roles and how many?

Compare with Part A:

- To what extent is each formal role matched with the expertise needed to fulfill the role's purpose effectively?
- To what extent is each team matched with the expertise needed to fulfill the team's purpose effectively?

Team Design Tool

Team Agreements

	Fixed	Flexible
Objective • Outcome-based objectives • Process-based objectives		
Team Composition • Transparency of selection • Strategic teaming (matching expertise and dispositions to the task)		
Key Activities • Decisions • Actions • Dispositional		
Logistics • Meeting duration, frequency, and schedule • Meeting attendance • Meeting roles • Between-meeting work		
Support • Time • Skill-building support/feedback • Access (to data, info, key people, etc.) • Compensation		
Communication • Within the team • From the team • With others engaged in the same leadership functions		

Role Design Tool

Role Analysis

Intended Outcomes Which specific groups of students will be affected? How?	Intended Outputs Which specific teachers will be influenced? How?	Key Tasks or Activities What will the teacher leader do to achieve these results?

Teacher Leadership Role Description

TEACHER LEADERSHIP ROLE DESCRIPTION
Role Title:

ROLE SUMMARY

Purpose

Provide a description of this role's purpose by identifying the leadership function(s) it addresses and by connecting, where possible, to specific school or district goals.

Role

Provide a brief summary of the primary tasks of this position. Writing this task summary may be easier after defining the responsibilities of the position (below).

ESSENTIAL RESPONSIBILITIES

List each main area of responsibility and give examples of the types of tasks that those responsibilities might entail. Required duties and deliverables should be described separately using clear and concise language.

Areas of Responsibility

Required Duties and Deliverables

Reports to

Teacher Leadership Role Description continued

TEACHER LEADERSHIP ROLE DESCRIPTION

QUALIFICATIONS

Identify the knowledge, skills, and/or abilities required for the satisfactory performance of the position. Then provide the minimum qualifications for the position, such as work experience, formal training, education, certifications, and/or licensures.

Knowledge, Skills, and Dispositions

Required	Preferred

QUALIFICATIONS

Education, Training, and Experience

Teacher Leadership Role Description continued

TEACHER LEADERSHIP ROLE DESCRIPTION
SUPERVISION
Provide a summary of the type of support and evaluation that the grade-level team leader can expect to receive. Also, describe how and when the position will be evaluated. **Support**   **Evaluation**
SELECTION AND LENGTH OF SERVICE
Provide a brief summary of the selection process, and describe the term limits for the role.
COMPENSATION
Describe the compensation, if any, for the performance of this role.

Meeting Agenda Template

Access this template in GoogleDocs at https://goo.gl/bRi5am

MEETING [#]–DATE			
Team Purpose			
Meeting Norms		**Meeting Roles**	
Meeting Attendance			

Schedule

Time	Min.	Activity	
		Check in	
		Review objectives for this meeting	
		Review next steps from previous meeting	

	Person Responsible	Task	Anticipated Completion Date
	All members	*This table and the text it contains are copied from the end of the previous meeting's agenda.*	

Meeting Agenda Template continued

Time	Min.	Activity
		Review plus (+)/delta (◻) summary from previous meeting
		Objective 1 Purpose: Process: Next steps: Notes:
		Objective 2 Purpose: Process: Next steps: Notes:

Meeting Agenda Template continued

Time	Min.	Activity
		Review next steps from this meeting

Review next steps from this meeting

Person Responsible	Task	Anticipated Completion Date
All team members	*What ideas and decisions from this meeting must be reported to other school teams?* We use this first row to capture anything from the meeting that we'd like to report back. Members are in the habit of copying this row into their own CPT agendas.	Next CPT

Be sure to carry over any continuing tasks from last time.

Notes:

Assess what worked well and what we want to improve

+ (What worked well)	☐ (What to improve in future meetings)/questions
• • • •	• • • •

Norms monitor's reflection:
• Which were hard for us today?
• Which helped us to be productive?

Facilitator's reflection:
• What was your personal leadership goal?
• What were the tricky parts of this meeting for you as a facilitator?

Meeting Agenda Template continued

Time	Min.	Activity
		Plan agenda for next meeting

Date: **Location:**

Facilitator:

Objectives:

1.

2.

3.

4.

Year-Long Planning Calendar (see https://goo.gl/TW43hK)

Appendix B

Resources for Extending Your Learning Together

Deepen your understanding and engage your colleagues in further conversation about chapter themes using these articles, tools, and books.

For each chapter, you will find

- *Ready Resources.* Open-access articles and tools that you can download and use now with your team.
- *Recommended Readings.* Book title suggestions that are worth purchasing if you want to dig deeper into chapter themes.

Chapter 1: Leadership as Influence

Ready Resources	Suggestions for Use
Overcoming the Obstacles to Leadership (Susan Moore Johnson & Morgaen. L. Donaldson) *Article (5 pages)* Accessible from ASCD's *Educational Leadership*: http://www.ascd.org/publications/educational-leadership/sept07/vol65/num01/Overcoming-the-Obstacles-to-Leadership.aspx	This short downloadable article can be an effective catalyst for an important conversation that leadership teams must have about the "triple threat" to teacher leadership—autonomy, egalitarianism, and deference to seniority—and about the supports and structures needed to avoid them. This article is one of 14 worthwhile articles in this themed issue of *Educational Leadership* addressing the topic of "Teachers as Leaders." The entire issue is available from ASCD.
Distributed Leadership: An Interview with Dr. Alma Harris *Article (4 pages)* Accessible from *Teacher* magazine: https://www.teacher-magazine.com.au/articles/distributed-leadership	This short article provides a concise overview of what distributed leadership is and describes key advantages and challenges. When teams examine this article together, they understand that although leadership is already distributed in schools, it is possible and even important to think more deliberately about the distribution of leadership. This comes from *Teacher* magazine, the journal of the Australian Council for Educational Research. Although articles in this open-access journal generally focus on the Australian context, the ideas are often equally applicable in the U.S. context, and subscribing to the free e-bulletin is worthwhile.
Success at the Core: Instructional Expertise Learning Module *Learning module* Accessible from Teaching Channel: https://www.teaching-channel.org/instructional-expertise-module-sac	This 120-minute professional learning module, complete with video segments, module handouts, and facilitator's guide, can support a team's efforts to identify and share instructional expertise throughout their school. Video segments illustrate the module's strategies for identifying and tapping teachers' expertise in the context of differentiated staffing, observation pairs, and coaching. The "Instructional Expertise" module is one of seven modules in *Success at the Core*, a video-based, downloadable professional development toolkit for teachers and leadership teams developed by Educational Development Corporation and accessible from Teaching Channel.
Recommended Readings	**Strategic Connections**
Connecting Teacher Leadership and School Improvement By Joseph Murphy Corwin, 2010	Readers who are interested in learning more about how teacher leadership has been defined, and about the key barriers and opportunities of teacher leadership, will appreciate this research-based volume.
Leader of Leaders: The Handbook for Principals on the Cultivation, Support and Impact of Teacher-Leaders By Hal Porter and William E. Collins Pearson, 2014	This is one of very few books written for principals about teacher leadership. It has an important chapter that addresses "principal paradigm shifting" and the work principals must do to change their perspective on their own role. It also addresses leaders' role in supporting a culture shift throughout the organization.

Chapter 2: Shared Vision

Ready Resources	Suggestions for Use
What Teachers Should Know and Be Able to Do *Booklet (52 pages) and video* Accessible from the National Board for Professional Teaching Standards (NBPTS): http://accomplishedteacher.org/	This downloadable booklet (and/or accompanying two-minute video) can prompt team members to think together about the important question: "What do we believe our community should expect of its teachers?" By critically and collaboratively examining the NBPTS Five Core Propositions, team members can compare and contrast their own assumptions and perceptions about teaching—and thus develop a shared vision while deepening respect and regard for each other. True professions have "standards of care" that allow the public to have confidence about what they can expect from that profession's members. The teaching profession had no such national standard, until the late 1980s when the NBPTS convened teachers and other education leaders to establish these "Five Core Propositions" for what every teacher should know and be able to do. The collection of 25 standards documents, also available from this website, describe what the five core propositions look like at an accomplished level within each grade span and content area.
Success at the Core: Leadership Teams and Quality Instruction *Learning module* Accessible from Teaching Channel: https://www.teaching-channel.org/instructional-expertise-module-sac	This 120-minute professional learning module, complete with video segments, module handouts, and facilitator's guide, can support a team's efforts to develop and maintain a shared instructional focus within their school. Video segments illustrate the module's strategies for strategic teaming, setting and assessing learning targets, and setting norms that keep the team focused on improvement. The "Leadership Teams and Quality Instruction" module is one of seven modules in *Success at the Core*, a downloadable, video-based professional development toolkit for teachers and leadership teams developed by Educational Development Corporation and accessible from Teaching Channel.
Shaping a Vision of Academic Success for All Students *Video-based learning module* Accessible from PBS Learning Media: https://mass.pbslearningmedia.org/resource/wall15.pd.lead.vision/shaping-a-vision-of-academic-success-for-all-students/	Chapter 2 addresses creating a shared vision for *instruction*. Your vision for instruction depends on your school's vision for *student learning*. This 12-minute video and supporting discussion questions can guide a team in developing a shared vision of the process of establishing a shared vision for student learning. The video features one school's journey, and the provided discussion questions support members to explore their own thinking about key aspects of the process so that they can get on the same page before beginning this collaborative work. The module is part of a five-part series on "School Leadership in Action," funded by Wallace and available from PBS Learning Media.

Chapter 2: Shared Vision continued

Ready Resources	Suggestions for Use
Developing a Shared Vision *Video* Accessible from ASCD: http://www.ascd.org/ascd-express/vol5/510-video.aspx	This resource link from *ASCD Express* (Vol. 5, Issue 10) offers a four-minute video and transcript of Rick DuFour and Karen Dyer providing three tips for engaging the community in establishing a school vision. Teams might use this as part of their effort to educate the community about what to expect during the vision-setting process and to reinforce their openness to rethinking existing structures and cultural norms. The archive of this free bimonthly themed newsletter has many additional volumes that may be useful for providing right-sized text for teams to explore together.

Recommended Readings	Strategic Connections
Shaping School Culture By Terrence E. Deal and Kent. B. Peterson Jossey Bass, 2016 (3rd edition)	This classic guide is a worthwhile book study for leadership teams as they embark on the process of refining a school's vision. It offers practical strategies for homing in on the unique values of your own community, articulating the vision for teaching and learning, and sharing responsibility for that vision throughout the community. A team can use this book to consider the formal and informal roles all can play in upholding that vision.
Data, Data Everywhere: Bringing All the Data Together for Continuous School Improvement By Victoria L. Bernhardt, Ph.D. Routledge, 2015 (2nd edition)	Who gets to share in a shared vision? Ultimately the vision must serve students and put them on a path of improvement. This volume can provide teams with more insight into using multiple data sources, as presented in Figure 2.6, and practical strategies for doing so. In fact, it includes a chapter specifically on creating a shared vision with data.

Chapter 3: Leadership Co-Performance

Ready Resources	Suggestions for Use
Group Juggle *Interactive activity* Accessible from: http://schoolreforminitiative.org/doc/group_juggle.pdf	This interactive activity (20–30 minutes) provides an opportunity for group reflection on the dynamics and emotions of working together. Post-activity reflection questions help the group to process their experience and develop shared meaning about what it means and what it takes to work together. This is one of over 100 useful resources accessible from the protocol library of School Reform Initiative (http://www.schoolreforminitiative.org/protocols/).
Teacher Leadership Skills Framework *Booklet (7 pages)* Accessible from the Center for Strengthening the Teaching Profession: http://cstp-wa.org/teacher-leadership/teacher-leadership-skills-framework/	This downloadable booklet describes the knowledge, skills, and dispositions that teacher leaders need by categorizing them into five skills sets. It is a worthwhile exercise for teams to review each set critically, consider the provided vignettes collaboratively, and consult together about the reflection questions. This is one of four useful tools available on this webpage. The others include A *Teacher Leader Self-Assessment* to support teacher leaders in setting and reflecting on professional growth goals, a *School and District Capacity Tool* to support systems leaders to assess the readiness of their contexts to support teacher leadership, and a reference tool describing the *Mathematics Knowledge of Content and Pedagogy* necessary for leading math-related initiatives.
The 2015 Professional Standards for Education Leaders *Recorded webinar* Accessible from the National Association of Secondary School Principals (NASSP): https://www.nassp.org/professional-learning/online-professional-development/archived-webinars/the-2015-professional-standards-for-educational-leaders	This webinar recording (one hour; slides downloadable) from January 20, 2016, led by Beverly Hutton and Mark Smylie, provides background on the development of the 2015 Professional Standards for Educational Leadership (PSEL), explains each standard in depth, and concludes with an informative Q&A session. Team members might review this resource individually before coming together to critically examine the PSEL standards, considering the implications for leadership co-performance, and comparing these national standards to their own local leadership standards. This resource is one of many archived webinars and other resources, including learning modules, available from the NASSP website.
TNTP: Teacher Talent Toolbox Online library of resources https://tntp.org/teacher-talent-toolbox	This open-source library of resources for strengthening instructional culture is populated with downloadable resources developed and used by educators from over 50 partner schools and districts. This indexed file cabinet includes topics such as Peer Culture and Collaboration and Teacher Career Progression.

Chapter 3: Leadership Co-Performance continued

Recommended Readings	Strategic Connections
Mapping Leadership: The Tasks That Matter for Improving Teaching and Learning in Schools By Richard Halverson and Carolyn Kelley Jossey-Bass, 2017	If the co-performance mapping activity in Figure 3.2 (and 1.2) intrigued you, this book may be of interest to you and your team. It introduces the research-based Comprehensive Assessment of Leadership for Learning (CALL) Framework—which outlines five domains of leadership important for learning with consideration for how these domains might be stretched across many people at a school.
Connecting Leadership with Learning: A Framework for Reflection, Planning and Action By Michael A. Copland and Michael S. Knapp ASCD, 2006	Similar to the *Mapping Leadership* title, this book offers yet another framework for thinking about the leadership functions most critical for learning. The framework can be used for evaluating one's own leadership practice, analyzing the distribution of leadership activity across leaders, and/or collaboratively examining provided cases with your leadership team.
Diagnosis and Design for School Improvement: Using a Distributed Perspective to Lead and Manage Change By James P. Spillane and Amy Franz Coldren Teachers College Press, 2011	Chapter 3 presents some simple tools to support leaders in paying more deliberate attention to how leadership is distributed in their schools. This volume will draw you in with a more in-depth and strategic approach to the same: diagnosing how leadership is currently distributed and designing strategic approaches to more deliberately maximize the human resources within your school.
How Teachers Become Leaders: Learning from Practice and Research By Ann Lieberman and Linda D. Friedrich Teachers College Press, 2010	This volume combines research with teachers' own narratives to draw new conclusions around four areas of teacher leaders' learning: how teachers develop a leadership identity, how they build collegiality and community, how they learn to make conflict productive, and how they learn from practice.
Collaborative Professionalism: When Teaching Together Means Learning for All By Andy Hargreaves & Michael O'Connor Corwin, 2018	Research and case studies from five countries inform this slim volume of key ideas for focusing professional collaboration on stronger outcomes for students.

Chapter 4: Culture of Teacher Leadership

Ready Resources	Suggestions for Use
Building a New Structure for School Leadership (Richard F. Elmore) *Booklet (42 pages)* Accessible from Shanker Institute: http://www.shankerinstitute.org/sites/shanker/files/building.pdf	In this publication from 2000, Elmore predicted, "If public schools survive [standards-based reform], leaders will look very different from the way they presently look, both in who leads and in what these leaders do." How far have we come since 2000? Teams that are intrigued by Chapter 4's ideas about teacher leadership as a culture of mutual responsibility may enjoy reading this booklet together and reflecting upon the current state of leadership in their context in light of Elmore's predictions.
Advancing Student Learning Through Distributed Leadership: A Toolkit for High School Leadership Teams *Toolkit (97 pages)* Accessible from the School Turnaround Learning Community: https://www.schoolturnaroundsupport.org/sites/default/files/resources/distributed_leadership_toolkit.pdf	Chapter 4 has a focus on role and team design. Teams that would like to dig deeper into this area may find this comprehensive downloadable guidebook helpful. It begins with an Action Step Checklist and includes chapters with ideas and tools for implementing each step, from selecting leadership team members, to defining a vision, to building capacity, to making data-informed decisions, to aligning structures and roles. Although the guidebook is written for high school leadership teams, the ideas are adaptable to schools with other configurations. This resource, from the Wisconsin Department of Education, is available on the website of the School Turnaround Learning Community, where many additional resources supporting shared and distributed leadership are available, as this is considered a key strategy for school turnaround.
Recommended Readings	**Strategic Connections**
Teaching in Context: The Social Side of Education Reform Edited by Esther Quintero Harvard Education Press, 2017	This book of nine essays presents multiple perspectives on a central issue underlying Chapter 4: how the organization of schools affects teachers, teaching, and learning. What helps teachers to feel committed to the profession, to excellence in their teaching, and to each other's excellence? Readers committed to the idea that teacher leadership is about culture, not about roles, will appreciate this volume. Teams might choose a chapter for collaborative reading and reflection.
Leading Change Together: Developing Educator Capacity Within Schools and Systems By Eleanor Drago-Severson and Jessica Blum-DeStefano ASCD, 2018	Similar to *Teaching in Context*, this book comes from the perspective that our context is important to how we know and learn (and do so together). It suggests that those who want to build educators' capacities, therefore, must be attentive to how schools are organized. The model presents four "pillar practices"—teaming, leadership roles, collegial inquiry, and mentoring—as well as recommended strategies for how we should talk to each other in those contexts to keep each other growing. Teams engaged in or interested in launching these practices will be well-served by this book.

Chapter 4: Culture of Teacher Leadership continued

Recommended Readings	Strategic Connections
Professional Capital: Transforming Teaching in Every School By Andy Hargreaves and Michael Fullan Teachers College Press, 2012	In traditional "egg crate" schools, individual teachers do their own work on their own every day, and when they retire, they take what they have learned with them. In this book, the authors advocate for teacher leaders and other school leaders to take a new stance. They call on us to recognize the power of our collective human, social, and decisional capital, and to devise ways to organize ourselves to benefit from each other's expertise more deliberately. Our individual accomplishments should become organizational assets. This is the power of professional capital, and it is a central theme of Chapter 4.
Leading Effective Meetings, Teams and Work Groups in Districts and Schools By Matthew Jennings ASCD, 2007	Chapter 4 presents some tools for designing teams in general. This book includes sections for particular types of teams. The section on inclusion teaching teams is especially useful. Readers who work in schools with inclusion classrooms know how challenging co-performance can be in these settings. Many adults working with the same students on different priorities and schedules can be a real problem if systems are not developed. This book has tools and guidance especially for such teams.
Becoming a School Principal: *Learning to Lead, Leading to Learn* By Sarah E. Fiarman Harvard Education Press, 2015	This book—not just for novice principals—is full of insights on the principal's role in ensuring teachers' voices and expertise are heard throughout the school.

Chapter 5: Strengthening Trust

Ready Resources	Suggestions for Use
Trust in Schools: A Core Resource for School Reform (Anthony S. Bryk & Barbara Schneider) *Article (5 pages)* Accessible from ASCD's *Educational Leadership*: http://www.ascd.org/publications/educational-leadership/mar03/vol60/num06/Trust-in-Schools@-A-Core-Resource-for-School-Reform.aspx	This short article introduces "relational trust," a composite of four types of trust—respect, personal regard, competence, and integrity—that the authors found to be a key common denominator in schools that improved and sustained those gains. The article describes the study from which these findings came and explains the important distinctions among the four types of trust. The Types of Trust Cards in Figure 5.2 are reprinted from this article. Readers may wish to read the full article together with their teams. This article is based on the core ideas from a much larger book by the same authors, *Trust in Schools: A Core Resource for Improvement* (Russell Sage, 2004).
Community Building Protocols *Online collection of protocols* Accessible from School Reform Initiative: http://www.schoolreforminitiative.org/tag/community-building/	This tagged collection includes over a dozen downloadable protocols for establishing the norms, community expectations, relationships, and routines that allow a group to build trust and feel safe enough to take the risks required for improvement. Readers will find these protocols invaluable to use, not only when establishing initial trust among members of a new team, but throughout the year to maintain and reinforce trust. This is one part of over 100 useful resources accessible from the protocol library of School Reform Initiative (http://www.schoolreforminitiative.org/protocols/).
Recommended Readings	**Strategic Connections**
Building Trust for Better Schools: Research-Based Practices By Julie Reed Kochanek Corwin, 2005	This book introduces the "Process Model for Building Trust" presented in Figure 5.4. It describes the research study from which this model came, and explains each component of the model supported by descriptive examples.
Trust Matters: Leadership for Successful Schools, 2nd edition By Megan Tschannen-Moran Jossey-Bass, 2014	Whereas the Bryk and Schneider model presented in Chapter 5 discusses four types of trust, this book introduces five types of trust. Readers may find it interesting to compare and contrast the two ways of thinking about trust. In addition, this book features chapters that are great for group study on building trust among colleagues, with families, and with students. It also has useful chapters that address betrayal and restoring broken trust.
Facilitating Teacher Teams and Authentic PLCs: The Human Side of Leading People, Protocols and Practices By Daniel R. Venables Corwin, 2018	Chapter 5 discusses the importance of creating an environment in which colleagues feel they can take the risks needed to learn. This book lays out key practices and protocols for creating such an environment. Complete with reproducible tools, diagnostic surveys, protocols, tip sheets, and vignettes for discussion, this book has everything one needs to get started. Importantly, it also warns of potential pitfalls and how to avoid them.

Chapter 6: Learning to Lead Together

Ready Resources	Suggestions for Use
Teacher Stories *Case studies* Accessible from the Center for Strengthening the Teaching Profession: http://cstp-wa.org/teacher-leadership/resources/teacher-stories/	Chapter 6 features three mini case studies. Case studies of teacher leadership enable teachers and administrators to work through awkward situations, tricky dilemmas, or true success stories in a way that is not personal. With this distance they can analyze what worked and where problems began. Teams might develop a routine of taking up a case study each month in an effort to get in sync about how a situation might be seen from various perspectives, as well as how it could be avoided. This webpage features 14 case studies from Volume 3 of stories from CSTP's 2016 summer writing retreat. More stories (as well as guidance on how to use them) can be found in the first volume, *Teacher Leader Stories*, listed below, under "Recommended Reading."
Leading from the Middle: Case Studies *Video case studies* Accessible from the New Zealand Ministry of Education: http://www.educationalleaders.govt.nz/Leadership-development/Key-leadership-documents/Leading-from-the-middle/Case-studies	These eight video cases (three to seven minutes each) are accompanied by a downloadable materials guide with video transcripts and discussion questions. The webpage was designed by the New Zealand Ministry of Education to be a resource for "middle leaders" such as coaches, mentors, and other teacher leaders. It can be a valuable resource for teams anywhere looking to practice collaborative analysis and problem solving with teacher leader case studies.
Recommended Readings	Strategic Connections
Examining Effective Teacher Leadership: A Case Study Approach By Sara Ray Stoelinga and Melinda M. Mangin Teachers College Press, 2010	This book is ready-made for study groups, with nine powerful vignettes that illustrate common teacher leadership dilemmas, together with research-informed activities, discussion questions, and suggested research for further reading. Teaching notes make it easy to navigate these materials and to customize them for your own group's needs.
Teacher Leader Stories: The Power of Case Methods By Judy Swanson, Kimberly Elliott, and Jeanne Harmon Corwin, 2011	This book can be a valuable resource for launching conversation among a mix of leaders. Three chapters present 16 cases in which teachers are leading from the classroom, outside the classroom, and beyond their schools. Another chapter provides teaching notes with references to the relevant teacher leader competencies (from the Center for Strengthening the Teaching Profession, also reprinted in Appendix C1).
School Systems That Learn By Paul B. Ash and John D'Auria Corwin, 2013	School and district administrators who want to take a deeper dive into understanding the work they need to do to support effective co-performance of leadership will appreciate this book of guidance from Ash and D'Auria. It lays out, in a clear and accessible way, how to create a "learning school system" characterized by trust, collaboration, capacity building, and shared leadership at all levels of the system.

BIBLIOGRAPHY

Adams, C. M., & Forsyth, P. B. (2013). Revisiting the trust effect in urban elementary schools. *The Elementary School Journal, 114*(1), 1–21.

Bacharach, S. B., Bamberger, P., & Mitchell, S. (1990). Work design, role conflict, and role ambiguity: The case of elementary and secondary schools. *Educational Evaluation and Policy Analysis, 12*(4), 415–432.

Berg, J. H. (2003). *Improving the quality of teaching through National Board Certification: Theory and practice.* Norwood, MA: Christopher Gordon Press.

Berg, J. H. (2007). *Resources for reform: The role of board-certified teachers in improving the quality of teaching* (Unpublished doctoral dissertation, Harvard Graduate School of Education).

Berg, J. H. (2010). Constructing a clear path to accomplished teaching. *Theory into Practice, Journal of Ohio State University's College of Education and Human Ecology, 49*(3), 193–202.

Berg, J. H., Bosch, C. A., & Souvanna, P. (2013, December). Critical conditions: What teacher leaders need to be effective in schools. *JSD, Learning Forward's Journal, 34*(6), 26–30.

Berg, J. H., Carver, C. L., & Mangin, M. M. (2014). Teacher leader model standards: Implications for preparation, policy and practice. *Journal of Research on Leadership Education, 9*(2), 195–217.

Berg, J. H., Charner-Laird, M., Fiarman, S., Jones, A., Qazilbash, E., & Johnson, S. M. (2005). *Cracking the mold: How second stage teachers experience their differentiated roles.* Paper presented at the annual meeting of the American Educational Research Association, Montréal, Québec, Canada.

Berg, J. H., Connolly, C., Lee, A., & Fairley, E. (2018). A matter of trust. *Educational Leadership, 75*(6), 56–61.

Berg, J. H., Miller, L. R., & Souvanna, P. (2011, June). Boston shifts learning into high gear: Certificate program accelerates student learning by building teacher capacity. *JSD, Learning Forward's Journal, 32*(3), 32–36.

Berg, J. H., & Zhao, J. (2017). *Inventory of teacher leadership programs: Pilot study.* Boston: University of Massachusetts.

Berg, J. H., & Zoellick, W. (2017). *Toward a more empirically useful conception of teacher leadership.* Paper presented at the annual meeting of the American Educational Research Association, San Antonio, Texas.

Bernhardt, V. L. (1998). *Multiple measures.* Oroville: California Association for Supervision and Curriculum Development.

Bryk, A.S., & Schneider, B. (2002). *Trust in schools: A core resource for improvement.* New York: Russell Sage Foundation.

Bryk, A. S., & Schneider, B. (2003). Trust in schools: A core resource for school reform. *Educational Leadership, 60*(6), 40–45. Retrieved from http://www.ascd.org/publications/educational-leadership/mar03/vol60/num06/Trust-in-Schools@-A-Core-Resource-for-School-Reform.aspx

Bryk, A. S., Sebring, P. B., Allensworth, E., Easton, J. Q., & Luppescu, S. (2010). *Organizing schools for improvement: Lessons from Chicago.* Chicago: University of Chicago Press.

Center for Strengthening the Teaching Profession. (2009). *Teacher leadership skills framework.* Retrieved from http://cstp-wa.org/teacher-leadership/teacher-leadership-skills-framework/

Center for Teacher Quality, National Board for Professional Teaching Standards, and National Education Association. (2014). *The teacher leadership competencies.* Retrieved from http://www.nbpts.org/wp-content/uploads/teacher_leadership_competencies_final.pdf

Chemers, M. (1997). *An integrative theory of leadership.* Hillsdale, NJ: Lawrence Erlbaum Associates.

Commonwealth of Massachusetts. (1994). *The Massachusetts Common Core of Learning.* Retrieved from https://archive.org/details/massachusettscom0mass

Copland, M. A., & Knapp, M. S. (2006). *Connecting leadership with learning: A framework for reflection, planning, and action.* Alexandria, VA: ASCD.

Daly, A. J., Finnigan, K. S., & Liou, Y. (2017). The social cost of leadership churn: The case of an urban school district. In E. Quintero (Ed.), *Teaching in context: The social side of education reform.* Cambridge, MA: Harvard Education Press.

Danielson, C. (2007). The many faces of leadership. *Educational leadership, 65*(1), 14–19.

Danielson, C. (2015). *Talk about teaching! Leading professional conversations.* Thousand Oaks, CA: Corwin.

Datnow, A., & Castellano, M. E. (2001). Managing and guiding school reform: Leadership in success for all schools. *Educational Administration Quarterly, 37*(2), 219–249.

Dweck, C. S. (2006). *Mindset: The new psychology of success.* New York: Random House.

Elmore, R. F. (2000). *Building a new structure for school leadership.* Washington, DC: Albert Shanker Institute.

Evans, L., & Teddlie, C. (1995). Facilitating change in schools: Is there one best style? *School Effectiveness and School Improvement, 6*(1), 1–22.

Frost, D. (Ed.). (2014). *Transforming education through teacher leadership.* Madison, WI: Leadership for Learning.

Fullan, M. (2003). *The moral imperative of school leadership.* Thousand Oaks, CA: Corwin.

Fullan, M. (2007). *The new meaning of educational change.* New York: Routledge.

Goddard, R. D., Tschannen-Moran, M., & Hoy, W. K. (2001). A multilevel examination of the distribution and effects of teacher trust in students and parents in urban elementary schools. *The Elementary School Journal, 102*(1), 3–17.

Griffin, G. A. (1995). Influences of shared decision making on school and classroom activity: Conversations with five teachers. *The Elementary School Journal, 96*(1), 29–45.

Gronn, P. (2002). Distributed leadership. In K. Leithwood, P. Hallinger, K. Seashore-Louis, G. Furman-Brown, P. Gronn, W. Mulford, & K. Riley (Eds.), *Second international handbook of educational leadership and administration* (pp. 653–696). Dordrecht, Netherlands: Kluwer.

Hargreaves, A., & Fullan, M. (2012). *Professional capital: Transforming teaching in every school.* New York: Teachers College Press.

Hargreaves, A., & O'Connor, M. (2018). *Collaborative professionalism: When teaching together means learning for all.* Thousand Oaks, CA: Corwin.

Harris, A., & Muijs, D. (2004). *Improving schools through teacher leadership.* London: McGraw-Hill Education.

Hart, A. W. (1994). Creating teacher leadership roles. *Educational Administration Quarterly, 30*(4), 472–497.

High, R., & Achilles, C. M. (1986). An analysis of influence-gaining behaviors of principals in schools of varying levels of instructional effectiveness. *Educational Administration Quarterly, 22*(1), 111–119.

Hoy, W. K., & Tschannen-Moran, M. (1999). Five faces of trust: An empirical confirmation in urban elementary schools. *Journal of School leadership, 9*(3), 184–208.

Ingersoll, R. M., Sirinides, P., & Dougherty, P. (2017). *School leadership, teachers' roles in school decision making, and student achievement (CPRE working paper).* Retrieved from http://repository.upenn.edu/cpre_workingpapers/15

Johnson, S. M. (2005). The prospects for teaching as a profession. In L. V. Hedges & B. Schneider (Eds.), *The social organization of schooling* (pp. 72–90). New York: Russell Sage Foundation.

Johnson, S. M., Berg, J. H., & Donaldson, M. L. (2005). *Who stays in teaching and why? A review of the literature on teacher retention.* Cambridge, MA: Project on the Next Generation of Teachers, Harvard Graduate School of Education. Retrieved from https://projectngt.gse.harvard.edu/files/gse-projectngt/files/harvard_report.pdf

Johnson, S. M., & Donaldson, M. L. (2007). Overcoming the obstacles to leadership. *Educational leadership, 65*(1), 8.

Johnson, S. M., Kraft, M. A., & Papay, J. P. (2012). How context matters in high-need schools: The effects of teachers' working conditions on their professional satisfaction and their students' achievement. *Teachers College Record, 114*(10), 1–39.

Katzenmeyer, M., & Moller, G. (2009). *Awakening the sleeping giant: Helping teachers develop as leaders.* Thousand Oaks, CA: Corwin.

Kochanek, J. R. (2005). *Building trust for better schools: Research-based practices.* Thousand Oaks, CA: Corwin.

Kotter, J. P. (1999). *John P. Kotter on what leaders really do.* Cambridge, MA: Harvard Business Press.

Leithwood, K., Seashore, K., Anderson, S., & Wahlstrom, K. (2004). *Review of research: How leadership influences student learning.* Retrieved from http://www.wallacefoundation.org/knowledge-center/Documents/How-Leadership-Influences-Student-Learning.pdf

Little, J. W. (1990). The persistence of privacy: Autonomy and initiative in teachers' professional relations. *Teachers College Record, 91*(4), 509–536.

Louis, K. S., Leithwood, K., Wahlstrom, K. L., Anderson, S. E., Michlin, M., & Mascall, B. (2010). *Learning from leadership: Investigating the links to improved student learning.* St. Paul, MN, and Toronto, Canada: Center for Applied Research and Educational Improvement/University of Minnesota and Ontario Institute for Studies in Education/University of Toronto.

Mangin, M. M., & Stoelinga, S. R. (2008). Teacher leadership: What it is and why it matters. In M. M. Mangin & S. R. Stoelinga (Eds.), *Effective teacher leadership: Using research to inform and reform* (pp. 10–35). New York: Teachers College Press.

Margolis, J., & Deuel, A. (2009). Teacher leaders in action: Motivation, morality, and money. *Leadership and Policy in Schools, 8*(3), 264–286.

Marks, H. M., & Nance, J. P. (2007). Contexts of accountability under systemic reform: Implications for principal influence on instruction and supervision. *Educational Administration Quarterly, 43*(1), 3–37.

Marzano, R. J., Waters, T., & McNulty, B. A. (2005). *School leadership that works: From research to results.* Alexandria, VA: ASCD.

McLaughlin, M. W., & Talbert, J. E. (2001). *Professional communities and the work of high school teaching.* Chicago: University of Chicago Press.

Miranda, H. P., Mokhtar, C., Tung, R., Ward, R., French, D., McAlister, S., & Marshall, A. (2014). *Opportunity and equity: Enrollment and outcomes of black and Latino males in Boston Public Schools.* Providence, RI: Annenberg Institute for School Reform at Brown University. Retrieved from http://www.annenberginstitute.org/publications/opportunity-and-equity-enrollment-and-outcomes-black-and-latino-males-boston-public-sch

Nadler, R. T., Rabi, R., & Minda, J. P. (2010). Better mood and better performance: Learning rule-described categories is enhanced by positive mood. *Psychological Science, 21*(12), 1770–1776.

National Board for Professional Teaching Standards. (n.d.). NBPTS | Shaping the profession that shapes America's future. Standards for NBPTS. Retrieved from http://www.nbpts.org/standards-five-core-propositions/

National Policy Board for Educational Administration. (2015). *Professional standards for educational leaders.* Retrieved from http://www.wallacefoundation.org/knowledge-center/pages/professional-standards-for-educational-leaders-2015.aspx

New Teacher Center. (n.d.). TELL Survey Initiative. Retrieved from https://newteachercenter.org/approach-old/teaching-empowering-leading-and-learning-tell/

Ovando, M. N. (1996). Teacher leadership: Opportunities and challenges. *Planning and Changing, 27*, 30–44.

Paulu, N., & Winters, K. (1998). *Teachers leading the way. Voices from the National Teachers Forum.* Washington, DC: U.S. Department of Education.

Pearce, C., & Conger, J. A. (2003). Shared leadership: Reframing the hows and whys of leadership. London: Sage.

Poekert, P. E. (2012). Teacher leadership and professional development: Examining links between two concepts central to school improvement. *Professional Development in Education, 38*(2), 169–188.

Quintero, E. (Ed.). (2017). *Teaching in context: The social side of education reform.* Cambridge, MA: Harvard Education Press.

Reynolds, D., & Teddlie, C. (2000). The processes of school effectiveness. In D. Reynolds & C. Teddlie (Eds.), *The international handbook of school effectiveness research* (pp. 134–159). New York: Routledge.

Ronfeldt, M. (2017). Better collaboration, better teaching. In E. Quintero (Ed.), *Teaching in context: The social side of education reform.* Cambridge, MA: Harvard Education Press.

Senge, P. (1990). *The fifth discipline: The art and practice of the learning organization.* New York: Currency Doubleday.

Sergiovanni, T. J. (1984). Leadership and excellence in schooling. *Educational Leadership, 41*(5), 4–13.

Silins, H., & Mulford, B. (2004). Schools as learning organisations: Effects on teacher leadership and student outcomes. *School Effectiveness and School Improvement, 15*(3–4), 443–466.

Smylie, M. A., & Denny, J. W. (1990). Teacher leadership: Tensions and ambiguities in organizational perspective. *Educational Administration Quarterly, 26*(3), 235–259.

Southworth, G. (2005). Learning-centered leadership. In B. Davies (Ed.), *The essentials of school leadership* (pp. 91–111). Thousand Oaks, CA: Sage.

Spillane, J. P. (2006). *Distributed leadership.* San Francisco: Jossey-Bass.

Spillane, J. P., Hopkins, M., Sweet, T. M., & Shirrell, M. (2017). The social side of capability: Supporting classroom instruction and enabling its improvement. In E. Quintero (Ed.), *Teaching in context: The social side of education reform.* Cambridge, MA: Harvard Education Press.

Supovitz, J. A. (2008). Instructional leadership in American high schools. In E. M. Camburn, S. M. Kimball, & R. Lowenhaupt (Eds.), *Effective teacher leadership: Using research to inform and reform* (pp. 144–162). New York: Teachers College Press.

Supovitz, J. A., Sirinides, P., & May, H. (2010). How principals and peers influence teaching and learning. *Educational Administration Quarterly, 46*(1), 31–56.

Teacher Leadership Exploratory Consortium. (2011). *Teacher leader model standards.* Carrboro, NC: Author. Retrieved from https://www.teachingquality.org/content/teacher-leader-model-standards

TNTP. (n.d.). Introduction to Insight. Retrieved from https://tools.tntp.org/confluence/display/INSIGHT/Introduction+to+Insight

Togneri, W., & Anderson, S. E. (2003). Beyond islands of excellence: What districts can do to improve instruction and achievement in all schools—A leadership brief. Washington, DC: Learning First Alliance.

Tschannen-Moran, M. (2004, November). *What's trust got to do with it? The role of faculty and principal trust in fostering student achievement.* Presented at the annual meeting of the University Council for Educational Administration, Kansas City, MO.

Tschannen-Moran, M. (2014). *Trust matters: Leadership for successful schools.* San Francisco: John Wiley & Sons.

Urban Education Institute, University of Chicago. (n.d.). Illinois 5Essentials Survey. Retrieved from https://illinois.5-essentials.org/2017/

Weiss, C. H., & Cambone, J. (1994). Principals, shared decision making, and school reform. *Educational Evaluation and Policy Analysis, 16*(3), 287–301.

Wenner, J. A., & Campbell, T. (2017). The theoretical and empirical basis of teacher leadership: A review of the literature. *Review of Educational Research, 87*(1), 134–171.

York-Barr, J., & Duke, K. (2004). What do we know about teacher leadership? Findings from two decades of scholarship. *Review of Educational Research, 74*(3), 255–316.

INDEX

Note: The letter *f* following a page number denotes a figure.

ABOUT THE AUTHOR

Jill Harrison Berg is a leadership coach and school improvement consultant. With Jill's support as a critical friend, professional learning leader, and strategic planning partner, education leaders are able to strengthen their capacities for creating powerful, coordinated systems that maximize the leadership potential of teachers.

Jill also consults with various local, statewide, and national institutions on matters of research and policy. Since 2013, she has served as a faculty member for the Network to Transform Teaching, a networked improvement community of cross-stakeholder teams representing 10 states that was convened by the National Board for Professional Teaching Standards to apply Carnegie's principles of improvement science to learn together how to bring accomplished teaching to every student every day. Currently, she is also co-principal investigator on a research study under way through the Consortium for Policy Research in Education to explore the range of ways programs across the United States support and develop teachers as leaders and to examine the impacts of such programs. Other institutions that have tapped Jill's expertise include the Massachusetts Department of Elementary and Secondary Education, Washington's Center for Strengthening the Teaching Profession, Educational Development Corporation (EDC), WestEd, and the National Research Council.

Jill has been an educator of leaders at all levels. She began her career in the classroom, with a passion for teaching elementary and middle grade students to be leaders who take ownership of their own learning and strive to be a positive influence on the learning of others. After earning National Board Certification, she left the classroom to pursue a doctorate, and continued to support the development of teacher leaders and other school leaders through various institutions of higher education and nonprofit organizations, including the Boston Plan for Excellence, Teachers21, Simmons College, Brandeis University, and the University of Massachusetts in Boston.

Throughout more than 25 years working in educational practice, research, and policy, Jill has written many articles on the topics of teacher leadership, teaching quality, and leadership development, and is the author of *Improving the Quality of Teaching Through National Board Certification* (Christopher-Gordon Press, 2003). She earned her doctorate at the Harvard Graduate School of Education while working as a researcher with the Project on the Next Generation of Teachers. She also holds a B.A. from Harvard University and an M.Ed. from Lesley University, and she was one of the first teachers in Massachusetts to become a National Board Certified Teacher (1998).

WHOLE CHILD
TENETS

The ASCD Whole Child approach is an effort to transition from a focus on narrowly defined academic achievement to one that promotes the long-term development and success of all children. Through this approach, ASCD supports educators, families, community members, and policymakers as they move from a vision about educating the whole child to sustainable, collaborative actions.

Leading In Sync relates to the **engaged**, **supported**, and **challenged** tenets.
For more about the ASCD Whole Child approach, visit **www.ascd.org/wholechild.**

1 HEALTHY
Each student enters school healthy and learns about and practices a healthy lifestyle.

2 SAFE
Each student learns in an environment that is physically and emotionally safe for students and adults.

3 ENGAGED
Each student is actively engaged in learning and is connected to the school and broader community.

4 SUPPORTED
Each student has access to personalized learning and is supported by qualified, caring adults.

5 CHALLENGED
Each student is challenged academically and prepared for success in college or further study and for employment and participation in a global environment.